HEART OF AN APOSTLE

Pete Beck

MASTER PRESS

New York

Heart of an Apostle © Copyright 2008

Published by:

Master Press
An Imprint of Morgan James Publishing
1225 Franklin Ave. Ste 325
Garden City, NY 11530-1693
Toll Free 800-485-4943
www.MorganJamesPublishing.com

ISBN# 978-1-60037-103-5

DEDICATION

To Earl E. Kellum, my friend and mentor, who is now with the Lord, and who embodied and demonstrated the true heart and spirit of the apostle.

CONTENTS

Preface: 7

Introduction: 9

PART ONE: THE HEART OF AN APOSTLE

Chapter 1: Apostles From the Inside Out 15

Chapter 2: Attitudes Toward the World 19

Chapter 3: Signs and Wonders 23

Chapter 4: Imparting of Gifts 25

Chapter 5: Authority 27

Chapter 6: Wisdom 35

Chapter 7: Lifestyle 39

Chapter 8: Sowing Spiritual Things 45

Chapter 9: Attitude Toward Churches 47

Chapter 10: Bringing Joy to the Church 51

Chapter 11: Confidence in Christ 53

PART TWO: HONORING FATHERS

Chapter 12: Why We Need Fathers 59

Chapter 13: Blessings and Curses 65

Chapter 14: Why Was David Blessed?.. 73

PART THREE: PROBLEMS WE GENERATE

Chapter 15: Honoring Sons 83

Chapter 16: Meekness and Gentleness 87

Chapter 17: The Grace of Being Teachable....................................93

Chapter 18: Devilish Ambition..99

Chapter 19: Moving Landmarks...105

Chapter 20: The Mystery of Lawlessness 109

Chapter 21: The Need for Help 115

Chapter 22: Vertical Versus Horizontal 123

Chapter 23: The Elijah to Jehu Anointing....................................127

Conclusion: 133

PREFACE

My dear Roman Catholic friends have a devotion to the "Sacred Heart" of Jesus. The idea itself is not a bad one. Jesus is Himself the Great and only True Apostle and the purposes of His heart should be of greatest concern to us. Our hearts certainly matter to Him. Did God not say that man looks at the outward appearance, but God looks at the heart? Therefore it behooves us to have a real concern for the heart attitude and condition of our leaders and ourselves. Our God is always looking. There is no place to hide!

Apostles are in vogue. Suddenly apostolic networks are springing up all over the earth. Much of this is the Holy Spirit's doing. But as with any surge of God's revelation and restoration of His government, there will be excesses of the flesh, misunderstanding by men, as well as efforts by Satan to intervene. Men have a way of getting some of what the Holy Spirit is saying and running with it. That is because we only see partially. None of us have it exactly right. God knows our frame. Thanks be to God that He is merciful. Though merciful, He really does expect us to be humble and teachable. If our hearts are right, the Lord will continue to lead and perfect us and consider us, like David, a man after His own heart.. As David said in Psalm 25, the Lord will teach us in the way.

This book endeavors to point out the heart that an apostle, or for that matter, any Christian leader should have is one that God is searching for daily. God is looking constantly for a man or woman to stand in the gap for His people and His purposes. There are many other books that deal with apostolic strategy and leadership techniques, the application of apostolic doctrine to the church and the like. Many of them do this better than I probably could. But I haven't seen any exhortations on the very core of the ministry, the heart. This is such an effort.

Please read on!

INTRODUCTION

"The refining pot is for silver and the furnace for gold, but the Lord looks at the hearts." (Prov 17:3)

Restoration of Apostles

We are living in a unique period in human history, the last days. As we hear what God's Spirit is now saying to the Church we begin to understand the special calling on this present generation. Much has been written and spoken in our day regarding the restoration of the ministry of apostles to the church. A flurry of books on the subject covering everything from apostolic authority, networking, apostolic church planting, and apostolic relationships have appeared on Christian bookshelves. Yet there is a certain danger inherent in these books that may subtly go unnoticed. They have almost exclusively focused on the apostolic office and its function. The danger is that apostles and their ministry are viewed from the point of view of their function only.

This book differs from other books on the subject in that it deals with what I believe is the real heart of a true apostle. It does address such things as apostolic authority, practical relationships between apostles and churches, and other topics, but the emphasis is on the heart.

How God views matters is to be found in 1 Samuel 16:7:

"But the Lord said to Samuel, "Do not look at his appearance or at the height of his stature, because I have refused

> *him. For the Lord does not see as man sees; for man looks at*
> *the outward appearance, but the Lord looks at the heart."*

Furthermore, the desire of God for restoration of spiritual heart relationships in the last days is further revealed by Malachi 4: 5 and 6. These are the last words of the Old Testament. They are a springboard over the gulf of 400 years to the birth of our savior, the Lord Jesus Christ.

> *"Behold, I will send you Elijah the prophet Before the com-*
> *ing of the great and dreadful day of the Lord. And he will*
> *turn the hearts of the fathers to the children. And the hearts*
> *of the children to their fathers, Lest I come and strike the*
> *earth with a curse."*

We can count on the Holy Spirit of God to set the stage in these last days for this prophecy to fully come to pass. He will turn the hearts! As a matter of fact, it is happening before our very eyes. Heart relationships of spiritual authority are coming into existence as never before. Men and women of good will are everywhere trying to get things right. In the hearts of many is a desire created by the Holy Spirit to have better meaningful relationships.

Relationship: The Basis For True Apostles

As these chapters progress it will become obvious that a major emphasis in this book is the importance of a heart relationship. Everything God does in His kingdom is based on relationship, both with God and with one another. It all begins with a relationship to Christ through the new birth. The parable of the vine and the branches teaches it. He demonstrates it in His relationship to the Father and the Holy Spirit.

Much damage has been done in recent years by so-called apostles attempting to oversee individuals and churches without establishing proper relationships first. When crisis comes (and it always does) the absence of real relationship between these apostles and the individuals and churches they are overseeing usually has a devastating effect on situations which might have been different had proper relationships first been established.

Relationships Do Not Rest On Authority, but Authority On Relationships

A dangerous precedent in recent years exists in over-focusing on the authority of apostles. Relationships do not rest on authority, but authority on relationships. There is no doubt that an apostle holds an important authoritative role in the church as Scripture indicates. In an age of rebellion and anarchy such authority needs once again to be emphasized. Yet an undue focus on an apostles' authority and function without a corresponding emphasis on the heart of the apostle has created an entire set of apostles who more closely resemble corporate CEO's than what is modeled in the New Testament. Claiming the apostolic mantle, they have missed the essence of the heart that goes with the office. Many in their zeal to see apostolic ministry restored, have neglected this simple basic reality. The damage has been great when men with a true apostolic call and gifting begin to treat the body of Christ as their own possession or view themselves as monarchs.

When Constantine rescued the church from Roman persecution at the beginning of the fourth century, the hierarchical model of oversight became the rule in churches. This was the form of government modeled in the Empire and seemed natural to them. This precipitated the hierarchical structure of the Roman Catholic and Greek Orthodox churches. It was carried on by the reformers, who were more concerned at that time with purity of doctrine and practice than with the structure of government. Since the world governments of that day were also monarchical, it was natural for this to be what the reformers saw as normal. Today the Holy Spirit is showing us another way.

The only remedy for avoiding the mistakes of the past and present is to recapture the true essence of the apostle and God's pattern for leadership. In this book the emphasis is not on what the apostle does, but on who the apostle is in Christ. When this is properly modeled, individuals and churches should have no problem receiving and working with such individuals. It is only when this relational aspect is ignored that apostles become corporate executives or at worse, tyrants. When this happens, churches will inevitably pull away from that which God intended as a channel for blessing.

> *"I know your works, your labor, your patience, and that you
> cannot bear those who are evil. And you have tested those
> who say they are apostles and are not, and have found them
> liars" (Rev. 2:2)*

In this passage from Revelation, the Lord commended the church at Ephesus for their discernment of true and false apostles. If we are to follow the Lord in this and receive his commendation, we also must be able to recognize and test true and false apostles. When we come to scripture there are many evidences given of what true apostles are like and how they should behave. We will now examine carefully the marks of a true apostle pulling from Scripture a biblical portrait of this all-important ministry.

It is important to take a moment here to say that some dispute the existence of the calling and office of apostle in our day. I sat with an apostolic man in Cairo, Egypt several years ago. He looked incredulous as I spoke of apostles. He had been taught that there were no such men or women outside of the twelve of the Gospels. I showed him in the scriptures that there were not only the apostles of the Lamb (Rev 21:14), but that there were others like Paul, Barnabas (Acts 14:14), Titus (2 Cor 8:23), Epaphroditus, (Phil 2:25) and Andronicus and Junia (Rom 16:7). In fact, if Ephesians 4 is interpreted correctly, there will always be apostles until we all come into the unity of the faith. Obviously this has yet to occur.

As I write this, I have a deep awareness of how much Christ really loves His Church. After all, He died for her (Eph 5:25). She is indeed the most precious and important thing on earth to Him and He will eventually come for her. Anyone with any kind of spiritual responsibility must look at her with an apostle's heart, endeavoring to present her a chaste virgin to her Divine Bridegroom. That is what God is calling for today in those who are truly apostles. May it be so!

PART ONE:

THE HEART OF
AN APOSTLE

1

APOSTLES FROM THE INSIDE OUT

"Then you shall again discern between the righteous and the wicked, between one who serves God and one who does not serve Him." (Malachi 3:18)

Much has been written recently defining the apostle by his function. Much has also been written defining the office by looking at historical models and shadows in the Old Testament. There are plenty of good books already written in this vein. Rather, I would like to discern what characterizes an apostle from the inside out. What should be his recognizable heart motivation? What are the biblical marks of a true apostle?

There is no question that Paul equates being an apostle with being a father. In First and Second Corinthians Paul describes many aspects of the heart of an apostle. His first display of the apostles for us is in 1 Cor. 4:9 and the verses following. Then he finishes the picture in verse 15,

> *"For though you might have ten thousand instructors in Christ, yet you do not have many fathers; for in Christ Jesus I have begotten you through the gospel"*

firmly equating fathers with apostles. I treat this particular theme in much detail in my former book, Not Many Fathers.[1]

Before I proceed any further, I feel I should make the following distinction. I maintain that an apostle should certainly be a father. Some further justification for this statement will be found in Chapter 12. Without argument some fathers are pastors, as well as other five fold ministries. Are all fathers apostles? No. There are father-pastors shepherding churches. There are father-apostles exercising care and authority over pastors and churches. Not all ministers are fathers, but all apostles should be fathers.

Some of the traits of true apostles I have characterized as external and overt. These I refer to as the 'active' marks of the apostle. They are discussed in chapters two through four. They are discussed rather briefly as they have more to do with function than heart. Other traits might be classified as 'inward' or internal; that is, they lie within the heart. Yet while they lie within they do produce an outward witness to those who observe the apostle over a period of time. Therefore, I refer to them as the apostle's 'witness' and have devoted chapters five through eleven to describing them. They are dealt with in greater detail as they are the reason for this book.

Anyone calling himself an apostle (or called that by others) should have some measure of these qualities evident in his life and ministry. That is not to say that everyone who has the apostolic mantle will necessarily embody all of these to the greatest degree. Yet there must be some modicum of evidence of these qualities if he is to be judged a true apostle. All will not agree on who is and who is not an apostle. Even the apostle Paul was not considered an apostle by some (I Corinthians 9:1-2). This was undoubtedly due in part to the fact that he did not have a deep enough relationship with some, so that they were unable to see, judge and receive his apostolic character, gift and heart. In some instances it may have been the work of Satan. In any case we must be able to discern, like

[1] Published by Master Press, Knoxville, TN (1-800-325-9136)

the church at Ephesus, those who are true apostles in our midst as well as those who are not.

Christ endows His apostles with a large world vision. They gather, set in order and establish. Pastors have similar gifts that are applied to local assets. However, apostles are always looking over the horizon. They are pioneers. You will find them engaged in the next battle while the present one may be still raging. They appear to be never satisfied. They are given a general's view of the battlefield. This is why, in my opinion, they are set forth first in 1 Cor 12:28 in that great discussion regarding the relating of the members of the Body of Christ. It is because of their mandate to push forward the Kingdom. Their ministry and authority, when received, is for strengthening and building the church toward the coming of the Lord. It is not for managing local assets. Some seem to think they are set forth first to manage local assets. This is evidence of a controlling spirit. True apostles create vision and support leadership to marshal those local assets in the ongoing battle toward the final victory. The correct receiving of apostolic authority and input by local churches is a vital key to church growth.

CHAPTER

2

ATTITUDE TOWARD THE WORD

"But we have renounced the hidden things of shame, not walking in craftiness nor handling the word of God deceitfully, but by manifestation of the truth commending ourselves to every man's conscience in the sight of God."
(II Corinthians 4:2)

A true apostle should have the ability to teach and impart a good doctrinal foundation into a church (Acts 2:42; I Cor 3:9-10, Ephesians 2:20). This should not be confused with preaching ability. Preaching is a powerful gift and greatly to be desired, but I are talking about more than just stirring emotions and building up souls. Yet neither should we confuse it with the recitation of cold, sterile doctrine fit only for the intellect. Intellect speaks to intellect as deep calls unto deep. The spirit and the intellectual part of the soul both need to be touched. This is called the renewing of the mind. The foundational truth of God must however be set in place by the power of the Spirit, not the power of the intellect. The church is ultimately built upon the revelation of Jesus Christ. This can only come from and by the Holy Spirit. That is not ever to say that good doctrine is to be ignored or that the intellect is not important. A renewed mind is the whole aim of sanctification. But the Spirit and the Word must be combined so that the

Spirit is resident in the Word. In this way, the Spirit of God lays the foundation as He uses the apostle.

There Is Never Room For Personal Agenda

Paul says in 2 Cor. 2 :17 " For we are not, as so many, peddling the word of God; but as of sincerity, but as from God, we speak in the sight of God in Christ. (NKJ)" which is a parallel thought to the scripture quoted in the heading to this chapter. To preach or teach with a personal agenda of exercising one's gift so as to set up a circuit of repeat invitations to speak, or to gain admirers, is a peddler's attitude. The attitude of the apostle should fit his God given ability, which is to impart doctrinal foundation and to build apostolic vision in the leaders and the people. If he is indeed an apostle, he will have Grace for this task and should be careful not to dilute his efforts with some other motive. Our agenda can only be the agenda of Christ.

This ability combines the Gospel (I Corinthians 9:16-17 and 15:1-6) and all its elements with other foundational teaching. This would include repentance from dead works, faith toward God, the doctrine of baptisms, the laying on of hands, the resurrection of the dead and eternal judgment (Heb. 6:1-2). It also involves the revelation of the King and His kingdom. This is essentially what comprised the 'apostle's doctrine' referred to in Acts 2:42. Within these subjects a whole range of other topics are certainly available to be covered. The centerpiece is always however, that Jesus is the Messiah, He died on the cross for our sin, He rose again from the grave, and He is coming again. The other matters covered must always be taught within the physical and spiritual parameters of Scripture. When these parameters are widened, narrowed, or in any way not strictly observed (so that something is either added or taken away from scripture), it will inevitably endanger the faith of the believers, as well as the foundation of the church. There is never room for any man's personal agenda. The foundation will be skewed and God's blessing will never rest on it fully. God will not permit us to build anything lasting on a faulty foundation.

One might ask at this point, "What is the difference between the apostle and the teacher in these particular endeavors?" The answer is that there is little difference in quality or quantity. The teacher's gift enables him or her to bring clarity to Scripture in such a way that people gain better understanding and receive revelation. In doing so he strengthens the foundation. The difference between the apostle and the teacher is in the supernatural, governmental anointing of the apostle to set the foundation in place. The teacher does not have an overlying grace to place things in position with relevance to other things. Often he does not see the joining and interplay of prophetic input to the teaching input or the evangelistic input, or the pastoral input. The apostle is broad enough to bring these ministries together.

In many ways, the man called to be a pastor is similar to the apostle in his anointing. He is able to see things fit together in application to the welfare of the local church since he is gifted to see their effects in the church. I have often thought that the pastoral gift is simply local, whereas the apostolic is both local and trans-local. That is to say the pastor is primarily locally oriented, whereas the apostle is primarily Kingdom and multi-church oriented. In my travels, I have met many local pastors who are apostles in the making. In His time, God will spread their tents so that their influence will reach far beyond their own local sphere.

There is another observation that must be understood pertaining to the measure which God gives to each man (Eph 4:7). In Deuteronomy the Lord tells us that there are "captains of ten, fifties, hundreds and thousands" (Deut. 1:15). Some men are only captains of tens. They make wonderful home group leaders. Others are captains of fifties and hundreds and can handle the situations and duties that occur in smaller groups and smaller churches. They are not to be lightly esteemed, for they are just as important to the kingdom of God as the grandest pastor of the largest church in New York, London or Los Angeles. Others are captains of thousands. The Lord Himself knows our capacities. He will not allow a captain of thousands to be wasted unless there is some personal lack of cooperation with the Holy Spirit going on behind the scenes that limits God's willingness to use him. To put a captain of tens or hundreds over thousands would be cruel indeed. It is a good thing to realistically assess one's limitations. This is where an apostolic team covering is helpful.

The five-fold gifts are important and greatly complement each other. Yet the true apostle's vision is broader than the others. It includes an anointing to bring things together. It involves the anointing of the pioneer, the risk taker. It also entails an anointing, not only to place the foundation himself, but also to see that others are doing it properly. When allowed by local authority, he has an ability to make corrections in a faulty foundation and should be able to do so with a minimum amount of destruction and trauma to the church.

CHAPTER

3

SIGNS AND WONDERS

"... for no one can do these signs that You do unless God is with him." (John 3:2b)

Is it fair today to expect that apostles perform signs and wonders as they did in the early church? We won't say very much about this as it really falls in the realm of function. However, a few thoughts are in order here.

"And through the hands of the apostles many signs and wonders were done among the people. And they were all with one accord in Solomon's Porch." (Acts 5:12)

and,

"Then fear came upon every soul, and many wonders and signs were done through the apostles" (Acts 2:43)

Perhaps it will be helpful to first define signs and wonders. According to Thayer's Definitions of Strong's Concordance, a sign is as follows: "A sign, a mark, a token; a) that by which a person or a thing is distinguished from others and is known; b) a sign, a prodigy, a portent, that is, an unusual occurrence, transcending the common course of nature: 1) used of signs portending remarkable events soon to happen; 2) used of miracles and wonders by which God authenticates the men sent by him, or by which men prove that the cause they are pleading is God's cause.."

A wonder, according to the same source is "1) a prodigy, a portent; 2) a miracle; performed by anyone."It is clear from the record in Acts that healing, deliverance, salvation, and outpourings of the Holy Spirit followed the apostles wherever they went. The scripture makes it clear that the real purpose of these signs and wonders was to attend and verify the preaching of the word. And it is not a stretch to say that such signs should be occurring regularly to authenticate true apostles today. I say regularly in accordance with the following reasoning. While we can read the Book of Acts in approximately two to three hours, it covers about twenty-five or thirty years of activity. The miracles we see in Acts were not necessarily occurring daily. Neither did signs occur every time Peter or Paul preached or visited somewhere. Since the presence of the Lord was so abundant in the early church, there is no doubt that a sign like the deaths of Ananias and Saphira was very spectacular, but not necessarily a daily or even a yearly occurrence. As far as we know that particular sign only occurred once.

We do see many great miracles and signs occurring in the world today. If all these were compressed into twenty-eight chapters of a book we might get the impression that there is one occurring every second. However, this would not necessarily be the case. Though many signs and wonders do accompany modern apostles they are not all super-spectacular in nature, nor need they be to confirm the office. Yet that being said, there should be something supernatural and wonderful at times attending apostolic ministry. If there is nothing at all, we should stand back and wonder if there is indeed a real apostle at work!

CHAPTER

4

IMPARTING OF GIFTS

"And when Simon saw that through the laying of on the apostles' hands the Holy Spirit was given, he offered them money." (Acts 8:18)

In this passage in the book of Acts the apostles were sent to Samaria by the brethren at Jerusalem to supplement the work of the evangelist Phillip. While Phillip's powerful evangelistic ministry had brought them to Christ, the Holy Spirit had not yet fallen on the new believers there. When the apostles arrived they began laying hands on the believers who then received the baptism in the Holy Spirit. A similar occurrence is recorded in Acts 19:1-6 when Paul met the twelve men near Ephesus who were believers. After laying hands on them they also received the Holy Spirit and spoke with tongues and prophesied.

From the record in Acts it appears that people received the baptism in the Holy Spirit either directly from Christ (as at Pentecost) or at the hands of the apostles. This is by all means a special sign that should be a part of the apostolic equipment. Many should receive the Baptism in the Holy Spirit at the hands of true apostles.

Paul refers to a gift imparted to his young son Timothy when he had laid his hands on him:

> *"Therefore, I remind you to stir up the gift of God which is in*
> *you through the laying on of my hands."*
>
> *(II Timothy 1:6)*

Most likely he was referring to the same incident when the presbyters (elders) had laid hands on Timothy. Since Paul mentions it he was evidently present (I Timothy 4:14). The implication is that something special happened when Paul laid his hands on Timothy. Without belaboring the point, it is obvious that something real is imparted when an apostle lays his hand, by the Spirit, on a young leader. Whatever Timothy received he was called to stir it up especially in times of necessity. There was such a supernatural witness to whatever was imparted that Simon wanted it. He wanted it enough to offer to pay money for it.

CHAPTER

5

AUTHORITY

"The king's heart is in the hand of the Lord, Like the rivers of water; He turns it wherever He wishes." (Prov. 21:1)

All authority is from God (Romans 13:1). Without question the Bible teaches that the only rightful power within creation is ultimately that of the Creator. All authority on earth is delegated from above and man is accountable for its use, whether he believes this to be true or not.

Apostolic authority is delegated authority from Christ and is delegated for the purpose of building the church:

"For even if I should boast somewhat more about our authority, which the Lord gave us for edification and not for your destruction." (II Cor 10:8)

Apostolic authority is delegated from above and should be used only for building up and not tearing down. To flow properly and be effective it must be funneled through solid relationships. Otherwise it always results in legalism. It does not flow well out of position without the relationship. Paul said:

"Am I not an apostle? Am I not free? Have I not seen Jesus Christ our Lord? Are you not my work in the Lord? If I am not an apostle to others, yet doubtless I am to you. For you are the seal of my apostleship in the Lord. " (1 Cor 9:1-2)

Governmental Versus Ministerial Apostles

I think we all recognize the existence of apostolic oversight and authority. But we can see from the above verse that it exists in some cases and not in others. The exercise of authority is based on involvement and serving, not on position. He who would be great is to be a servant. However, there is "governmental apostleship" based on such relationship and involvement which has to be recognized and agreed to by the saints being governed. The apostle is not responsible to make authority work, the Lord is! Moses fell on his face and turned it over to God when he was confronted with the rebellious! The saints are responsible to God for recognizing God's authority in an apostle or father. Witness what happened to Korah and his brethren! Since true submission to authority can only come from the heart, a solid relationship of trustworthiness and friendship has to be in place. There is also a "ministerial apostleship" which does not have to involve any oversight whatsoever. Recognizing someone as having the gift of an apostle does not necessarily confer authority over lives and situations .

Alexander the Great

Plutarch tells a story about Alexander the Great. Alexander lived from 356 to 323 B.C. He is recognized as one of the greatest leaders of all time. He conquered and exercised tremendous authority over most of the known world before he died at the age of 33. This story is retold by Bill Bennett[1] and illustrates how authority is fulfilled and flows in service and relationship rather than position.

"Alexander the Great was leading his army homeward after his great victory against Porus in India. The country through which they now marched was bare and desert and his army suffered dreadfully from heat, hunger, and, most of all

---

[1] The Moral Compass, William J Bennett, Simon and Schuster, 1995, New York, NY, page 657.

thirst. The soldiers' lips cracked and their throats burned from want of water, and many were ready to lie down and give up.

About noon one day the army met a party of Greek travelers. They were on mules and carried with them vessels filled with water. One of them, seeing the king almost choking from thirst, filled a helmet and offered it to him.

Alexander took it in his hands, then looked around at the faces of his suffering soldiers, who craved refreshment just as much as he did.

"Take it away," he said, "for if I drink alone. The rest will be out of heart, and you have not enough for all."

So he handed the water back without touching a drop of it. And the soldiers, cheering their king, leaped to their feet, and demanded to be led forward."

This type of leadership is a far cry from those who would exhibit their credentials by riding in expensive cars and demanding to be put up in four star hotels, as some do. Even though the apostle must sometimes "root out and pull down" as well as bring correction, the motive behind godly authority is always to encourage and build up the church and its people. If correction is not followed up by encouragement and rebuilding, it is doubtful that authority was properly exercised.

There Is A Measure, It Is Not Unlimited

Authority is also limited. Paul says as much in 2 Cor 10:13-15:

> *"We, however, will not boast beyond measure, but within the limits of the sphere which God appointed us—a sphere which especially includes you. For we are not overextending ourselves (as though our authority did not extend to you), for it was to you that we came with the gospel of Christ"*

Notice Paul mentions "not boasting beyond measure, but remaining within the limits of the sphere" God had appointed him. To go beyond the measure of one's authority is to be ambitious for self. It is always demonic in nature and

29

eventually produces a negative reaction in the body of Christ. Paul ends chapter ten of Second Corinthians with the admonition, "But he who glories, let him glory in the Lord, For not he who commends himself is approved, but whom the Lord commends (2 Cor. 10:17-18). **Seeking for authority** beyond one's measure (or what the Lord has clearly given) is always an attempt at self-glorification. It is the basis of false apostleship about which we are warned in Revelation 2:2.[2] Self-promotion is clearly Satanic in principle and lies at the heart of Satan's own attempt at self-exaltation above the throne of God.

It goes without saying that to boast beyond one's measure is also evidence of the flesh. Contrast that with Paul's own testimony regarding the manner in which he walked while among the Corinthians:

> *"For our boasting is this: the testimony of our conscience*
> *that we conducted ourselves in the world in simplicity and*
> *godly sincerity, not with fleshly wisdom but by the grace of*
> *God, and more abundantly toward you. For we are not writ-*
> *ing any other things to you than what you read or under-*
> *stand. Now I trust you will understand, even to the end."*
> *(2 Cor. 1:12-13)*

What a difference between the way the apostle carried himself while with them and those super-apostles who had seduced them by their own boasting and self-aggrandizement! Simplicity and godly sincerity demanded that the apostle walk humbly, not boasting in himself and his own achievements in contrast to those false apostles whose authority was based in their own fleshly claims.

We Will Not Have Dominion Over Your Faith

This heart attitude included the refusal on Paul's part to attempt to control others or interfere with their faith:

---

[2] If you think about it, it is also the basis of much false prophecy. The attempt at self-glorification is present in some prophetic attempts. These go beyond what God has indeed authorized. As we approach the end, God must deal severely with false prophets. We must be found innocent of ambition when speaking for God.

" Not that we would have dominion over your faith, but are
fellow workers for your joy: for by faith you stand"
(2 Cor. 1:24).

Paul understood that every individual in the Body of Christ must walk by his or her own faith, for this is the only way to Christian maturity and to pleasing God. "The just shall live by his faith" is the central theme of the Bible. According to Paul, this is the role of the apostle (and for the rest of the five-fold ministry); that through them the church might be brought to maturity so that it pleases God in every way (Eph. 4:13-15). To exercise dominion over anyone's faith is to hold them back from maturing in the same way that a parent who keeps a child from stumbling and falling down hinders that child from learning to walk.

In the passage quoted above, Paul makes it clear that the goal of ministry is to be fellow-workers promoting the saint's joy, while refusing to take dominion over their faith. While he deals strongly with the Corinthians' sins in no uncertain terms, even exercising authority to turn a sinful man over to Satan, he does not take dominion over their faith. His way is to send them word, hoping that upon hearing they will be obedient (2 Cor. 2:9).

Now this was certainly a risky affair. What if the church had not responded? The fact is they did respond. The foundation that the apostle had laid was good. He could also trust that the Holy Spirit would witness to his words and work in the hearts of the people and their leaders. A great deal more about this will be said in Chapter 11 under the heading of Confidence in Christ.

Too many times I have seen apostolic fathers rush in at the first sign of major trouble, take the authority out of the hands of the local leadership and attempt to control the outcome. This may seem like the safest way to protect apostolic reputation, but it is certainly not the Pauline way. It also is not the way of insuring that the saints achieve maturity.

Years ago, during a severe governmental crisis in a wonderful church I was asked to help out and had authority to do so. I was receiving phone calls almost daily from outside brethren who had an interest in the outcome. Some of these calls were rather intimidating in nature and insisted that I "do something." One call came late one night from a prophetic brother who had quite a bit of clout in the Christian world as well as influence in our situation. He told me that "everything was falling apart, that if I didn't do something he was going to step in, find someone with some authority, and get something done, and that if it all fell apart, that I was going to get the blame." I told him as calmly as I could that it was apparent from his own statement that he recognized his own lack of authority if he had to "find someone", and that it would probably be better if he stayed out of the whole situation. One thing I have found to be true over the years is that rebellion always feeds on "supposed" authority. When there is division there is usually real authority versus some kind of supposed or pseudo authority.

I already knew of a godly solution working in the wings and within a few days the Lord supplied the answer to the crisis and everyone saw the Lord's hand at work rather than my hand. This increased their faith. When the answer became obvious I then had to take some action to put it into effect, but nevertheless it was clearly the Lord's answer. The people are always strengthened when they see the Lord work. They are also more willing in the long run to follow leaders who demonstrate that they can hear the Lord and are willing to forbear and let Him work.

When men rush in to take over churches with deep problems, changing pastors and elders abruptly and arbitrarily, they damage people's faith as well as relationships. There are many churches no longer in existence because of this kind of brash action on the part of apostles. This is due in part to the fact that some apostolic men are so afraid of failure and the possible damage to their own reputations that they move too quickly to abort churches. They will only give their real serious time and effort to successful churches so as to avoid any risk of failure. This is the easy way, but it is not truly caring for churches.

Only God has the right to put a church to death since only He can bring it to birth. In the case where a church is sick or in danger, the apostle's job is to hold its hand; not to pull the life support plug himself. Obviously there may come a time to walk away, but Christ will make that abundantly clear when that time has arrived. There should never be any guessing.

I have seen so-called apostolic men hide failures in their relationships, their endeavors and in their ministries. Men will often hide their failures in their marriage and church relationships. Why? For fear of what others will think if they discover it. This, of course, is not God's way. God is not afraid to reveal the failures of key men in Scripture such as David and Peter. Paul also revealed the relational breaches he had with Demas and Alexander the Coppersmith (2 Tim 4:10; 14). It is true that gossip is forbidden and that "where there is no wood the fire goes out" (Prov 26:20). The only reason to cover something is when it will damage another to reveal it. But is never right to hide things when those from whom they are hidden are part of the solution to the problem. Apostolic teams and church leadership must be open and above board with each other if their authority is to remain in tact.

Young People Need To See That Leaders Are Open

If our pride is not in the way and we are not trying to impress men then we have nothing to hide. If we are truly not subservient to the approval of men, then we will not be bothered greatly by their disapproval. Young men are actually strengthened by seeing leaders that are human, who occasionally fail, are open, repent with humility and continue to lead with even greater humility. Failure can be a tremendous teacher. They are strengthened by seeing their leaders learning from their mistakes and continuing with Christ. This demonstrates the mercy and grace of our Lord. It demonstrates the humility of the leader and his dependence on the Lord. Authority is actually weakened when leaders hide their failures out of pride or fear of losing their position. A demonstration of confidence and faith is worth more than a teaching on the same.

" Thus also faith by itself, if it does not have works, is dead. But someone will say, "You have faith, and I have works." Show me your faith without your works, and I will show you my faith by my works." (Jas 2: 17-18)

CHAPTER

6

WISDOM

"According to the grace of God which was given to me, as a wise master builder I have laid the foundation." (I Cor 3:10)

"The wise in heart will receive commands, But a prating fool will fall." (Prov 10:8)

There are certain word groupings whose order is repeated where ever they are found in Scripture. These terms are meant to relate together in a certain order and God wants us to see how they relate. For instance, mercy and truth are constantly related together with mercy always preceding truth (2 Sam. 15:20; Ps 25:10; 85:10, 86:15. 89:14; Pro. 3:3, 14:22, 16:6 and 20:28).[1]

Similarly, **wisdom and understanding** are joined together throughout the entire Bible (Ex. 36:1; Deut 4:6; 1 Kings 4:29, 7:14; 1 Chron. 22:12; Pro. 1:2, 2:6, 3:19, 4:5, 4:7, 8:1, 8:14, 24:3; Isa. 11:2; Dan. 1:20, Col. 1:9). I shall show

---

[1] There is one exception to this rule found in Micah 7:20. The reason is easily discerned, but has no bearing on what we are discussing in the theme of this section of this chapter.

later how wisdom is the chief attribute or characteristic of the true apostle which is joined to understanding which is the chief characteristic of true prophets.

Look at what the apostle Paul says about himself in 1 Cor. 3:9-10:

> *"For we are God's fellow-workers; you are God's field, you are God's building. According to the grace of God which was given to me, as a **wise master builder** I have laid a foundation, and another builds on it. But let each one take heed how he builds on it. (Emphasis mine)*

Notice his reference to the wisdom that God had given him for building God's house. We shall see that wisdom is the chief characteristic with which true apostles must be endowed from above.

In the five-fold ministry the ministries of apostles and prophets are the key for foundational building. That is why they are always listed first and second in the two major lists of ministries in the New Testament (I Cor. 12:28, Eph. 4:11). When these two "house-building" ministries are viewed in the context of another text from the Old Testament we are able to understand more fully each one's role in building God's house:

> *"Through wisdom a house is built, and by understanding it is established. By knowledge the rooms are filled with all precious and pleasant riches." (Prov. 24:3-4)*

Since God states clearly in this text that both wisdom and understanding are required to build a house, we can better understand what each (apostles and prophets) brings to the process. Since apostles are first in foundational building and wisdom is the chief element necessary in establishing a house, it stands to reason that wisdom must be the chief mark of an apostle while understanding that of a prophet.(I am speaking here of the office rather than the gift) That is not to imply that an apostle has little or no understanding and the prophet has no wisdom. It simply means that a man who is a called apostle must demonstrate a consistent and unusual measure of wisdom. While wisdom alone is not the only characteristic of apostles, it is certainly the chief one.

What is the relationship between apostles and prophets with teachers? It is alluded to in the above citation. Teachers pour in knowledge only when there is a container, the foundation and the walls. Another Scripture that might shed light on this is found in Proverbs 3:19-20:

> *"The Lord by wisdom founded the earth, by understanding He established the heavens; By His knowledge the depths were broken up, and clouds drop down dew"*

A Container is Needed to Keep Knowledge from Being Poured On the Ground

The apostle and prophet build the walls of wisdom, understanding and heavenly revelation. These walls keep out the enemy and keep in the knowledge that is poured into the house by the teaching gift. Without wisdom and understanding, knowledge is rather dangerous. Only when apostolic wisdom and prophetic understanding are imparted into the foundations and walls, can they be safely filled with knowledge from the teacher. Only then can the rooms be filled with "all precious and pleasant riches." Only then can five-fold teaching be effective in building the church.

Knowledge "puffs up" (I Cor. 8:1) if it is not contained within the walls and foundation of wisdom and understanding. Many questionable doctrines are presented to the Body of Christ in the myriad of books found today in Christian bookstores. Their veracity must always be measured and contained (or limited) by the walls built by wisdom and understanding. This explains why so many people and churches seem to drift off into humanism and strange doctrines as well as compromise. When an apostolic-prophetic foundation has not been laid, knowledge is not given the parameters it needs to be fruitful.

CHAPTER

7

LIFESTYLE

"According to the grace of God which was given to me, as a wise master builder I have laid the foundation, (Ps. 101:2)

"The wise in heart will receive commands, But a prating fool will fall." (Prov 20:11)

There are certain things we should know about a leader before we can have confidence in his or her leadership. The apostle Paul was not afraid to appeal to the things that his spiritual son Timothy knew about him as the evidence of his apostolic leadership:

"But you have fully known my doctrine, manner of life, purpose, faith, longsuffering, charity, patience, afflictions, which came unto me at Antioch, at Iconium, at Lystra; what persecutions I endured: but out of them all the Lord delivered me" (2 Tim. 3:10-11).

It is not difficult, if you know what questions to ask, to ascertain a person's doctrine and basic approach to Scripture. This can be achieved rather quickly. On the other hand, it takes time to discern whether or not a person is living out what he believes or is a hypocrite. Obviously, to "fully know" a person's manner of life, purpose, demeanor under crisis, stress, temptations, etc. as Timothy did Paul, requires an ongoing deep relationship with that person.

The lifestyle and demeanor of a father-apostle figure is extremely important in identifying the legitimacy of his calling. It is interesting to note that the early church had drawn up a written code of conduct called the 'Didache' by which churches could identify a true apostle or prophet. One of the first things the code dealt with was the issue of finances. If the so-called apostle or prophet personally asked for money it was considered as a sign that he was a false prophet or apostle.[1] That is amazing, especially in light of the obsession many ministers seem to exhibit today regarding money. While poverty is clearly no blessing and the idea that a minister should live at a poverty level is ridiculous, for a man of God to leave the impression that he has come for money is wrong. Yet how many give the impression that the emphasis is to collect money from God's people?

Paul certainly stresses in his letters that it is proper for churches to support apostolic ministry (2 Cor. 11:8-8, 1 Cor. 9:9-11, 1 Tim. 5:18). Yet when money becomes a motive for ministry it is a travesty. Paul reserved his severest rebuke in his letters for those who made this their emphasis:

> *"For the love of money is a root of all kinds of evil, for which*
> *some have strayed from the faith in their greediness , and*
> *pierced themselves through with many sorrows. But you, O*
> *man of God, flee these things and pursue righteousness, god-*
> *liness, faith, love, patience, gentleness" (1 Tim. 6:10-11).*

When this motive is operating it has the power to diminish and ultimately destroy relationships. That is why, in my opinion, the early church fathers included this warning about not receiving those who asked for money—they knew how

---

[1] See Early Christian Fathers, edited by Cyril C. Richardson, Collier Books, Macmillan Publishing Co. New Yor,, 1970: Didache, pages 176-177. This is an excellent work and is recommended along with The Early Christians, a Sourcebook on the Witness of the Early Church, by Eberhard Arnold, Baker Book House, Grand Rapids, Michigan, 1979.

potentially damaging such men would be to the church! In this light, we should always examine our own motives concerning money in the ministry.

The scripture clearly says that God has set forth apostles (fathers) as last of all (1 Cor. 4:9-16). This should not be confused with Paul's statement found later in the epistle that they are set as first in the church (12:28). The latter passage pertains to the place God has given the apostles governmentally and in servant leadership in the church. Though they are first in government they are also to be first in demeanor and presence, that is, in humility and suffering.

C. Gene Wilkes says "We who lead often overlook that the true place of Christlike leadership is out in the crowd rather than up at the head table."[2] How much better off the church would be if apostolic men could grasp this and learn to walk this tight rope, first in government, while being last in arrogance, covetousness, personal ambition, control, etc. They are last in privilege. They come under to serve while leading the church.

Unfortunately, the history of the church testifies for the past two thousand years to the abuses of power and position that have taken place through church leaders who should have been fathers. I just spent months restudying church history to prepare for a week of teaching on the subject for a missionary camp in Central America. The misunderstanding of and misuse of authority over the centuries has severely damaged the church in general and has chopped at the root of Christ's intended authority in the eyes of men everywhere.

In our day, the result of this misuse has been that many young leaders are afraid to fully submit themselves to apostolic oversight because of abuses they have seen or heard about and damaged relationships they have experienced. Apostles must strive to correct this so that the blessings can come upon young leaders and their churches.

How Do We Look Under Pressure?

Paul speaks in the above passage (2 Tim 3:10-11) about the persecutions he endured. This was a constant diet for these early apostles. Later, he reminds his son Timothy of the witness he maintained in these trials and how the Lord had delivered him out of them all. The question real apostolic fathers must face is, "What kind of face do we show the young men and our peers when the going

---

[2] C. Gene Wilkes, *Jesus on Leadership,* Tyndale House Publishers, Inc. Wheaton , IL 1998., This book is really worth reading and digesting by anyone who seriously wants to follow Christ and lead His Church.

gets really tough? Do we demonstrate faith when we walk through these trials or do we manifest uncertainty?" This is clearly one of the qualifications for those who would be fathers in the faith. I imagine that the young men with Paul were greatly strengthened in their resolve to serve Christ when, after being stoned and left for dead, Paul got up and went right back to the city to visit the brethren where he had just been persecuted. (Acts 14:20).

Fair Weather Apostles

In light of this we must be willing to ask ourselves some hard questions. What does it take to keep us from going forward for Jesus and His church? When we baby or unduly protect ourselves or turn aside from fulfilling obligations because of inclement weather or personal inconveniences? What kind of message do we communicate to the younger men and to the church? Are we willing to endure hardness for the sake of the Gospel? Do we protect our health, privacy or comfort beyond obeying God and instead of fostering relationships in the Body of Christ? Are we able to go when tired or mildly sick? Some I have known will not reside with the saints on ministry trips, but insist instead on hotel accommodations. Not only that, but they want four-star accommodations. Does this work to foster and build relationships? We must be prepared to see our own difficulties as opportunities to strengthen the church. This can be part of what is meant by 'enduring hardship for the sake of the Gospel'. Listen to what Paul said about his sufferings in his second letter to the Corinthians:

> *"Now if we are afflicted, it is for your consolation and salvation, which is effective for enduring the same sufferings which we also suffer. Or if we are comforted, it is for your consolation and salvation. And our hope for you is steadfast, because we know that as you are partakers of the sufferings, so also you will partake of the consolation"*
> *(2 Cor. 1:6-7).*

Apostles Must Absolutely Demonstrate That They Put People First, Not their Own Desires and Comfort.

One of the cultural aspects of America that has crept into the church, I am afraid, is a softness and unwillingness to put up with inconvenience. Many would rather be served than serve. We prefer expense accounts and nice restaurants rather than eating spaghetti around a kitchen table with the saints. We like privacy better than putting up with a lack of it to build a better relationship with some brother. We can't put up with noises, or snoring. Is it really better to get a good night's sleep than to better develop a relationship?

Some of the best and tightest relationships I have with brethren have come with a cost. That cost has been sleeping with the family's dog or cat romping across the bed in the middle of the night. It has meant sleeping in a hot room with no air conditioning. It has meant eating things I would rather not have eaten. It has meant sleeping in a dirty bed that smelled like stale sweat. It has meant spending hours just talking with hurting people in their living rooms and kitchens when I really would rather have been preparing for preaching, resting, or shopping, or napping, or what have you. It has meant going to a place several times and not having time to see the sights. I was in Mexico many times over a period of fifteen years before I ever saw Acapulco. Apostles must absolutely demonstrate that they put people first and not their own desires and comfort.

Faith is Demonstrated in the Crisis

It is vital that younger men see stability and steadfastness in apostles. We cannot play-act but must actually express faith when things go awry. A dear brother once expressed it this way; "Aaron put on his beautiful garments when he went out before the people; he only had on his linen garment when before the Lord in the Holy of Holies." Before the Lord, in private, we are given the privilege of complaining and weeping. Paul himself, our role model, said in 2 Cor 7:5 that he experienced fears within as well as pressures from without. Many of David's psalms attest to this inward turmoil. However, we must walk in an attitude of stability, confidence, and faith before the people. If we don't possess and demonstrate faith and stability in times of hardship and crisis, it may be that in reality we are not called to apostolic ministry.

In Gal 1:15-16 where Paul tells us about his calling, he expresses it thus:

" But when it pleased God, who separated me from my mother's womb and called me through His grace, to reveal His Son in me, that I might preach Him among the Gentiles...."

Note that his primary calling was to reveal Christ in him, his second assignment was to preach to the gentiles. Unless we show authenticity in our walk, preaching will be hollow. The example of the role model is first and foremost. Much of our loss of savor as salt to the world is directly due to the fact that we don't live up to what we preach. An apostle above all leaders must be true to this calling.

8

SOWING SPIRITUAL THINGS

" Incline my heart to Your testimonies, And not to covetousness. Turn away my eyes from looking at worthless things, And revive me in Your way." (Psalm 119: 36-37)

In this regard, the apostle must exhibit utter purity in his dealings with finances. An apostolic father sows spiritual things, not material things (1 Cor. 9:11). This same scripture allows him to reap material things, but not to sow them. It should cause great concern when we see purported apostolic men today drawing people and churches into business ventures and using kingdom relationships and influence for sponsoring, promoting, and selling various things. The apostle must be very careful with even appearances of sowing material things into the church. Mammon is the principality over our culture. Since greed is rampant in our culture, it must not even be named among apostles as well as any Christian leaders. Jesus laid down this basic axiom that one "cannot serve God and Mammon." We must never put ourselves in a light where people can for one moment feel as though we consider them as prospects, financial investors or customers instead of the precious sheep of Christ.

It is true that Deuteronomy 8:18 says that the Lord gives us power to gain wealth. This scripture has been used quite frequently to justify Christians manipulating others into business and financial ventures, sometimes to their sorrow. This scripture however shows that the purpose of the Lord in allowing us to gain wealth is that His covenant might be established. Making money is not a sin. The Body of Christ needs more entrepreneurs and solid businessmen who are willing to support the work of the Lord with their tithes and offerings.

To use one's influence and position as a five-fold leader in the church to manipulate people into investing in business ventures can lead to much damage in lives, pocketbooks and relationships. We must cultivate those who have a gift for producing money in a godly way. We must give them vision and trust the Lord to motivate them. We must sow spiritual things in their lives and let them by faith sow their material things into the Kingdom.

"Follow me as I follow Christ" Paul exhorted the Corinthians. I remember marveling at that statement when first reading it many years ago. At that time, I thought that Paul was either so far ahead of me that I would never catch up, or a supreme egotist. Yet as I matured, I understood that Paul was simply setting an example for the saints to follow. It is not by any means that Paul was perfect. Yet he was secure enough to know that to the best of his ability he was following Christ and therefore was not ashamed to ask men to follow him. At the end, he was able to say that he had run a good race and that a crown was laid up for him (2 Tim. 4:8). It should be the goal of every true apostle to be able to say the same thing.

CHAPTER

9

ATTITUDE TOWARD CHURCHES

"From following the ewes that had young He brought him, To shepherd Jacob His people, And Israel His inheritance. So he shepherded them according to the integrity of his heart, And guided them by the skillfulness of his hands."
(Psalm 78:71)

The apostle represents Christ and is an extension of Christ's ministry on earth. Christ loves the church and died to give Himself for her (Eph. 5:25). The true apostle feels no less inclined to live and die in the same manner. That is certainly the heart of the apostle Paul as witnessed by what he told the Corinthians:

"For I am jealous for you with godly jealousy, For I have betrothed you to one husband, that I may present you as a chaste virgin to Christ" (2 Cor. 11:2)

Many scriptures speak of the Lord's jealousy. The apostle feels the jealousy that the Lord feels for His own bride. That is not difficult to grasp. The best way to incur a man's wrath is to insult or molest his wife or fiancée. In ancient times, a king would have eunuchs to care for his harem as well as his wives to insure that their purity and chastity were preserved for the king. No one dared to touch his intended bride with lusty or unclean hands. If found out, his head would come off! That is to say, woe to those who touch the Bride of Christ with unclean hands! The Lord is jealous over His bride and will judge all that treat her carelessly or improperly.

As a father, the true apostle has this same desire to see Christ's bride, the church, pure and spotless. He is jealous for her in a godly way. The apostle Peter refers to those who by covetousness exploit the saints :

> *"By covetousness they will exploit you with deceptive words;*
> *for a long time their judgment has not been idle, and their*
> *destruction does not slumber." (2 Peter 2:3).*

In the Authorized Version, this passage is translated "making merchandise of the saints." We must watch our hearts and guard the flock in these last days against those who would sully the bride. The production of wealth seems to motivate a good deal of ministry we see on the national scene in these days. Making merchandise of the saints is an abomination!

We Must Watch Our Hearts

Another aspect of the apostle's heart for the church is his willingness to "spend and be spent" for it. (2 Cor. 12:15) He is not concerned with recognition or achieving esteem at the hands of the saints. While it is natural for a man to want to be well liked, this cannot rule the decisions that a true apostolic father makes. Sometimes to do what is right is not popular. To serve the Lord and the churches, willing to be spent, even if there is no immediate return, this has to be the heart of the apostle toward the churches. His ultimate approval comes from God, not from the people.

CHAPTER 9

This has practical implications for the apostle's relationship to the church and finances. Sometimes spiritual fathers subtly demonstrate a lack of integrity in this area. Some, while announcing that they live by faith, are tempted to return to those churches that give the largest offerings. Are the smaller churches to be ignored? Are they to be loved the less or served the less?

It is possible for a man to have an 'intellectual' love for the church or the Body of Christ in general, and not transfer that love to specific churches in a practical way. There are many in this world who say they love the poor, but do not express that love practically to poor individuals on a one on one basis. It is popular today to be in favor of helping the homeless. But to actually sacrifice oneself to actually help the homeless is another matter entirely. The true apostle will base his ministry on the commands of the Holy Spirit and not on the size of the offering.

> *"...besides the other things, what comes upon me daily: my deep concern for **all the churches"** (2 Cor. 11:28 emphasis added)*

Paul penned these words to a church that was having trouble with his apostleship. Yet he shows no signs of holding back love or ministry to them even though they were rejecting him. Anyone who has ever had to minister to those who rejected him knows how difficult it is. Yet Paul's apostolic heart would not succumb to pettiness or let a spirit of rejection cause him to hold back. Though he be loved the less, he continued to look for any crack through which he could pour his love.

> *"Open your hearts to us. We have wronged no one, we have corrupted no one, we have cheated no one. I do not say this to condemn; for I have said before that you are in our hearts, to die together and to live together" (2 Cor. 7:2-3)*

The apostle holds each individual church in his heart in the same way that a husband holds a wife. This should be expected if the apostolic office is just an extension of Christ Himself. It is a portion of His ministry, for He loves the church that way too. In a certain sense, the church has rejected Christ for the last two thousand years, yet He has never rejected her for one moment! Nevertheless, it grieves the Holy Spirit when leaders look at the church as a pawn in a power game or a way to make a living.

CHAPTER

10

BRINGING JOY TO THE CHURCH

"There are many who say, "Who will show us any good?"
Lord, lift up the light of Your countenance upon us. You have
put gladness in my heart, More than in the season that their
grain and wine increased." (Psalm 4:6-7)

"But they shook off the dust from their feet against them, and
came to Iconium. And the disciples were filled with joy and
with the Holy Spirit" (Acts 13:51-52)

This small but important chapter highlights one of the most subtle attributes of a true apostle.

The apostles Paul and Barnabas were traveling. Proclaiming that the Gospel was being brought to the gentiles and being rejected by the Jews, they arrived at Iconium. Joy was the result of their visit. Joy should accompany an apostle, for joy is a fruit of the Holy Spirit and evidence of the kingdom. In another passage, Paul speaks of the joy that the believers brought to him (2 Cor. 1:14).

If the church really believes the Gospel and sees the messengers modeling the Gospel, the automatic result should be joy. I am not speaking here of "silliness". It is unimaginable that Christ was ever silly. Silliness is never becoming to a minister of the Gospel. Paul speaks firmly against jesting which he says always leads to further ungodliness. I am convinced that any discerning Christian ought to be able to tell the difference between showmanship, silliness and performance and the true joy that comes from the real anointing which is the Holy Ghost. It is reported by the Holy Spirit that Jesus was filled with the "oil of gladness" above his fellows. Jesus was not a sourpuss. A sense of humor is a great thing if used within the parameters of godly propriety. Christians should as a general rule be the happiest people on earth. Happy is that people whose God is the Lord. (Psalm 144)

There should always be joy and encouragement attending the ministry of the apostle. I have had the privilege over the years of hosting as well as attending many church gatherings where true apostolic team ministry was present. I have never failed in thirty odd years to see real joy accompany these meetings. Within a few days of this writing, I attended such a meeting where real apostolic team ministry was present. It involved a gathering of about twelve churches and their leaders and people. At least three spiritually joined apostles were present with the sole purpose of bringing encouragement and feeding. The times of praise and spontaneous dancing before the Lord were a testimony to the real joy that was in that place. This type of thing should always occur when the true representatives of Christ tend to the flock. Fathers should bless the children. If we are to strengthen the churches, then joy has to be a result. The joy of the Lord is indeed our strength!

11

CONFIDENCE IN CHRIST

"Though an army may encamp against me, My heart shall not fear; Though war should rise against me, In this I will be confident." (Psalm 27:3)

*"Beloved, if our heart does not condemn us, then **we have confidence toward God**. And whatsoever we ask, we receive of him, because we keep his commandments, and do those things that are pleasing in his sight. And this is his commandment, that we should believe on the name of His Son Jesus Christ, and love one another, as he gave commandment."*
(1 John 3:21-23)

Having a firm confidence that Christ is in charge and knows what He is doing is the most critical thing for an apostle. The writings of the apostle John are absolutely unique in the New Testament. One of the reasons for the John's writings was to encourage confidence in God and His Son. As apostolic writings these letters reveal that at the heart of apostolic faith was utter confidence toward God inspiring others to believe in the faithfulness of the Lord Jesus Christ.

When things go wrong, how quickly some apostolic leaders take matters into their own hands. Evidence that leadership is really mature is that it really believes and acts like Christ owns the church and knows what He is doing. Confidence in Christ is needed. This is one quality that absolutely must be evident in those who are apostles. They cannot be men who talk about God's sovereignty and grace on one hand and deny it entirely by the way they live and act. They must not manipulate men and churches for their own end. Their modus operandi is to pray, teach, preach, exhort, setting an example for others to follow. They must have utter confidence that Christ will move on hearts and bring about the desired goal. They must have this confidence to the end and believe that He will save to the uttermost.

Such confidence was evident in the apostle Paul who said:

> *"And **we have confidence in the Lord concerning you**, both that you do and will do the things we command you. Now **may the Lord direct your hearts** into the love of God and into the patience of Christ"(2 Thess 3:4-5 emphasis added)*

Paul's reference to commands never carries with it the idea of manipulation, but rather exhortation. The Greek root from which the word is derived means "to enjoin" or to "give a message." Many other Scriptures can be cited to show Paul's complete confidence in Christ's ability to move in His Church to accomplish His desired end. Paul's own ability to trust God and Christ was crucial to the success of his ministry. To see the apostolic father truly confident in Christ breeds confidence in the children as well. It is no wonder that he was able to transfer that confidence in a measure to the saints in the various churches as evidenced by the following Scriptures:

> *"And I wrote this very thing to you, lest, when I came, I should have sorrow over those from whom I ought to have joy, **having confidence in you all** that my joy is the joy of you all"*   *(2 Cor 2:3 emphasis added)*

CHAPTER 11

*"Therefore I rejoice that **I have confidence in you in every-thing"**   (2 Cor 7:16 emphasis added)*

*"And we have sent with them our brother whom we have often proved diligent in many things, but now much more diligent, **because of the great confidence which we have in you.** "   (2 Cor 8:22 emphasis added)*

*"**I have confidence in you, in the Lord**, that you will have no other mind; but he who troubles you shall bear his judgment, whoever he is"   (Gal 5:10 emphasis added)*

*"**Having confidence in your obedience**, I write to you, knowing that you will do even more than I say" (Phile 1:21)*

Paul's obvious confidence expressed to these churches should not be construed to be confidence in human nature. Indeed, Paul had abundant experience to know the frailties of human beings and he was certainly not ready to trust them. Like His Master before him he also "knew what was in man" (John 2:24-25). Rather, Paul's confidence is in Christ and it is transferred to the elect because of his utter confidence that "he who has begun a good work in you will complete it until the day of Christ" (Philippians 1:6).

So often men preach publicly that Jesus will see them through and will never abandon them. Are they able to act it out?   Unlike their Lord and Paul they do not exhibit the same faith toward the brethren. Will we have the same confidence in Him with regard to the church and God's purpose to sustain those that are His?

Learn by Watching Dogs

On occasion I have had the privilege of watching a Scottish shepherd herd sheep with a trained sheep dog. The trained sheep dog achieves spectacular results by simply obeying the signals of the shepherd. This is a truly wonderful thing to watch. It is true that he has his own instincts and learns certain moves on his own within the parameters of his master's commands. I have heard of dogs actually running over the backs of the sheep to get to the other side of the flock in an emergency. Yet the sheep dog would never think of himself as the chief shepherd. His place is that of total obedience to his shepherd's commands. Having been with him since he was a pup, he has complete confidence that his master knows exactly what he is doing. The natural mind can never think or reason its way out of a spiritual dilemma. A spiritual dilemma is spiritual and not scientific. It is only when we obey that the darkness and obscurity begin to disappear. Obedience is the only way out of a spiritual dilemma, because only the Spirit knows the things of the Spirit.

In a certain sense, apostles as well as leaders in general are to be like these sheep dogs. They are simply called to fully obey their Master's command regarding the Church. To be a true apostle there must be quiet confidence in the One who said, "I will build my church and the gates of hell shall not prevail against it!" (Matt. 16:18). *The primary characteristic of a mature and godly leader is that he really believes that Christ is in charge.* What is more, he acts like it as well by obeying the commands of the Chief Shepherd. If he doesn't then he himself does not truly believe it and is therefore disqualified. It is only in the exercise of faith, which is never absent from obedience, that we can possibly please God.

PART TWO:

HONORING FATHERS

CHAPTER

12

WHY WE NEED FATHERS

"Hear, my children, the instruction of a father, And give attention to know understanding; For I give you good doctrine: Do not forsake my law. When I was my father's son, Tender and the only one in the sight of my mother, He also taught me, and said to me: "Let your heart retain my words; Keep my commands, and live. (Prov 4:1)

For the last several decades there has been a growing emphasis in the church on the restoration of the ministry of the apostle to the church. A growing number of churches and church movements have recognized their need for this foundational ministry to lead the way as the church approaches the time of the end. For those who are rightly called "apostles", the times are crucial. We shall see in part three of this book how much damage can be done by those in apostolic ministry who have not allowed the maturity of fathers to be the basis of their ministry.

When I speak about God giving the church fathers I am not speaking in a general sense about those who are teachers, preachers, or leaders. Thankfully, we have not had a shortage of gifted men who could minister in the church. Giftedness does not equate with maturity and fatherhood. When we speak of fathers, we are talking about God giving to the church more than gifted men. Fathers are those who have the heart of God for the church, that live not for their own blessing and purpose, but that God's people might be mature, lacking in nothing of the fullness of God.

The Scriptures have much to say about spiritual fathers and their importance to God's purposes. Spiritual fathers did not just appear with the death and resurrection of Christ and the creation of the Body of Christ. Even among God's people in the Old Testament there were spiritual fathers who played an important part in leading the nation of Israel. Under both covenants God has ordained spiritual fathers as an integral part of the life and blessing of God's people.

The Chain of Causation

Even before the Exodus, God's plan for Israel began with the fathers. God entered into a special agreement with the fathers of Israel in which He promised to do certain things for their descendants after them. On the eve of Israel inheriting the land of Canaan, Moses reminded their descendants why it was that God had delivered them from Egypt and was about to give them this good land:

> *"**Because he loved your fathers** and chose their descendants after them, he brought you out of Egypt by his Presence and his great strength, to drive out before you nations greater and stronger than you and to bring you into their land to give it to you for your inheritance, as it is today. Acknowledge and take to heart this day that the Lord is God in heaven above and on the earth below. There is no other. Keep his decrees and commands, which I am giving you today, so that it may go well with you and your children after you and that you may live long in the land the Lord your God gives you for all time."*   *(Deuteronomy 4:37-44 Emphasis mine)*

Moses clearly reminds Israel that these blessings were not due to anything that they had done or ever will do. Rather, their present and future blessings began with the fact that God loved their fathers! The chain of causation of God's plan for Israel begins with His love for the fathers. And because He loved them

He chose their descendants after them, promising to give them the land they were about to inherit. This is not to say that God does not also love the children, for God is love! But, His subsequent actions follow because He loved the fathers!

Through them the nation had its physical beginnings. Yet this idea of fatherhood has a much wider application than merely the physical. It is also used in a general sense for anyone who births something and brings it into being. In this sense, it is used of a whole host of people from politicians to founders of industry. We still refer to George Washington as the 'father' of our country. It is written that God made Joseph a 'father' to Pharaoh (Genesis 45:8). Orville and Wilbur Wright are rightly called the 'fathers' of modern aviation since they are attributed with being the founders of it. Simon Bolivar is often referred to as the 'father' of several South American nations.

One of the key things to note is that a man is said to be a 'father' when what he initiates continues to exist. No one today would say that Teddy Roosevelt is the father of the 'Bull Moose' Party for that political party no longer exists. A father is one who initiates something (a family, an industry, a nation, a church) and what he has initiated continues after he is gone. A 'fatherhood' refers to the beginning of some kind of life or vision that was initiated through an individual and continues to this day. What God the Father initiated will continue in existence. This is a definition of fatherhood.

Churches Have Fathers

As with nations and political systems, churches are initiated by fathers as well. A church is founded by God's anointing, gifting, and vision imparted through a person. The life of the Father is imparted to someone, creating vision in that individual. This is imparted to others and the result often is that a church comes into being. Such a person is often likened to a pioneer, willing to break new ground. Our own nation was founded by such pioneers; men and women with vision to move away from territory already settled in search of new lands to settle. Because of their vision they often inspired others to launch out with them. The result was that many areas of our own country, especially in the West, were discovered and the country rapidly grew.

Pioneers start churches. This was especially true of those first generation churches started by the apostles in the New Testament. These apostles were men who gave birth to new spiritual families. That is why the apostle was essentially the church planter in the First Century. The principle of life is in the father and as life flows through him things are initiated. In appealing to the Church at Corinth who were rejecting his apostolic authority. Paul reminds them that it was through him that they owed their existence:

> *"For it seems to me that God has put us apostles on display at the end of the procession, like men condemned to die in the arena. We have been made a spectacle to the whole universe, to angels as well as to men. We are fools for Christ, but you are so wise in Christ! We are weak, but you are strong! You are honored, we are dishonored! To this very hour we go hungry and thirsty, we are in rags, we are brutally treated, we are homeless. We work hard with our own hands. When we are cursed, we bless; when we are persecuted, we endure it; when we are slandered, we answer kindly. Up to this moment we have become the scum of the earth, the refuse of the world. I am not writing this to shame you, but to warn you, as my dear children. Even though you have ten thousand guardians in Christ, you do not have many fathers, for in Christ Jesus I became your father through the gospel. Therefore I urge you to imitate me. For this reason I am sending to you Timothy, my son whom I love, who is faithful in the Lord. He will remind you of my way of life in Christ Jesus, which agrees with what I teach everywhere in every church."*
>
> *(I Corinthians 4:9-17 KJV, Emphasis mine)*

Paul then bases his appeal on the fact of his relationship to them as a 'father. It was he who had first come to them with the Gospel (see Acts 18). This is the principle of initiation previously referred to. He is their father because he is their apostle—without him they wouldn't exist! Because Paul had begotten them they were his sons and therefore were duty bound to honor him.

When God begins to unfold His plan he first looks for those who are fathers. Because God loved their fathers we should not be surprised to find that he instilled in the consciousness of their descendants the absolute importance of honoring them. This is why the Commandments contain the clear command:

"Honor your fathers and mothers, so that it might be well with you" (Ex 20:12).

We must understand that to value what God values will bring blessing and prosperity. As each Israelite honored his earthly father God would bless them in very measurable ways. So important was this command that their well being depended on it.

Value What God Values

It is a divine principle applicable in every age. That is why in the New Testament we find the command to honor fathers repeated again yet with the added promise for those who obey it that they would "prosper and live long on the earth" (Ephesians 6:2). It is called the 'first commandment with promise.'

In First Corinthians, the apostle Paul reminds his converts that he alone has the authority to bring correction to them since his relationship to them is more than that of a teacher (I Corinthians 4:15). This passage reveals the heart of real apostolic ministry. Paul speaks from his "father" relationship with the church at Corinth as the basis of his appeal and the exercise of his authority. He expected them to understand that while God had blessed them with many gifted men, they had only one father in the faith. This establishes the important principle that fathers are not just gifted individuals, but those who have a special apostolic relationship with churches.

A Fatherless Generation

In both the Old and New Testaments fathers held a vital place in the life of God's people. But how should the modern church relate to fathers? Are they needed in today's church? And if so how do churches go about finding fathers they can relate to? The Church like the culture in which it exists has become increasingly fatherless. The absence of true fathers has meant that a major source of strength and blessing has been absent from the church. This will become more evident as we proceed.

Giant Killers

Saul's men never killed a single giant! That was because Saul never killed any, and he was their role model. On the other hand, David's men killed several giants in 2 Samuel 21. David was old and succumbing to physical weakness. His men came to the rescue and the chapter records how they killed several giants. This is a perfect picture of how young men take after their role models. To produce a giant killer, you have to be one. To produce a father, you have to be one.

CHAPTER

13

BLESSINGS AND CURSES

*"Therefore the Lord God of Israel says: 'I said indeed that
your house and the house of your father would walk before
Me forever.' But now the LORD says: 'Far be it from Me; for
those who honor Me I will honor, and those who despise Me
shall be lightly esteemed." (1 Sam 2:30 Emphasis mine)*

There is a distinct blessing to be had by honoring God the Father. There is
a transference of this blessing to those who also honor fathers. To be lightly
esteemed by God is the reverse.

First, we must honor fathers simply because God Himself has honored them.
The Word of God is full of statements of the honor that God expects fathers to
receive. One of the things that we must settle right up front is that we don't honor
fathers because they are perfect and have it all together. We honor them because
it is a commandment! This will become very clear as we study David's heart in
the next chapter. We have seen this in the story of the fathers of the nation of
Israel, Abraham, Isaac, and Jacob. The Holy Spirit does not shield us from the

reality of their lives but gives us a full account of their lives, warts and all! There was nothing special about these men apart from the operating grace of God working in their lives. God chose them and therefore He loved them. And because He loved them, He loved and chose their seed after them. That is why the New Testament says of their descendants:

> *"Concerning the gospel they are enemies for your sake, but concerning the election they are beloved for the **sake of the fathers**" (Romans 11:28, emphasis added).*

You and I are saved because God started something with our fathers. Since they are God's link of causation He demands that they be given their due respect.

Cursing Fathers

The book of Proverbs is full of statements about the proper relationship we must have towards our fathers. Proverbs was a sort of discipleship manual for the nation of Israel. The goal for every Israelite was the development of a heart of wisdom. Proverbs provided practical instruction in gaining a wise and discerning heart. And right at the forefront of such wisdom was the proper treatment of parents as those who gave us life.

> *"He who curses his father or his mother, his lamp will be put out in deep darkness" (Prov 20:20)*

> *"The eye that mocks his father and scorns obedience to his mother, the ravens of the valley will pick it out, and the young eagles will eat it." (Prov 30:17)*

Strong's Concordance gives the meaning of the word curse in the above scripture as "to make light of, to make small or trifling; to abate; to bring into contempt or despise; to lightly esteem." This differs from what we normally think of as cursing—chanting incantations over a boiling cauldron or some other thing associated with witchcraft. In fact, it is not even speaking ugly words directly against your father, although it could certainly include that. Any form of lightly esteeming fathers or making light of them in the heart is a form of cursing them and brings God's judgment.

The meaning of these proverbs is that the result of my making light in my heart of a father is that I will experience a lessening of revelation and understanding. If I don't repent, the inevitable result may be the extinguishing of all revelatory light so that I walk in total darkness. If this continues the result invariably is that I end up "walking in my own light" and this is disastrous. Witness what Isaiah says:

> *"Look, all of you who kindle a fire, who encircle yourselves*
> *with sparks:* ***walk in the light of your fire*** *and in the sparks*
> *you have kindled—this you shall have from My hand:* ***you***
> ***shall lie down in torment.****" (Is 50:11 Emphasis mine).*

It is necessary to have revelatory light from the Holy Spirit if we are going to build and lead the church properly since only the Lord is able to build the church. If we lightly esteem fathers, it is a sure way to diminish or cut off the light from above. Judging from all the problems, failures, and lack of fruit in the churches, many seem to be walking in their own light.

A man can imitate the anointing of God for a time. Many are fooled by a persuasive personality, misled by a leader with a strong soul and natural gifts. To the undiscerning these can masquerade as the real anointing. So many projects and plans may seem good to the natural or intellectual mind and may even seem to succeed for a season. Yet nothing will produce lasting fruit unless it is initiated as light from Christ and maintained by the Holy Spirit. And only lasting fruit glorifies the Father.

Spiritual Blindness and Pride

The light that comes from Christ casts no shadow. When we light our own fire we cannot help but cast a shadow. When we try to see by our own fire, there is always a shadow somewhere beyond us and our vision is impaired.

The quote from Proverbs 30:17 illustrates the same principle. Despising and mocking a parent will cause one to lose his eyesight. To be spiritually blind in these days is a most terrifying prospect

Proverbs also speaks of another aspect of blindness:

> *"There is a generation that curses its father, and does not bless its mother. There is a generation that is pure in its own eyes, yet is not washed from its filthiness" (Pro. 30:11-12).*

These verses speak of perhaps the most insidious form of spiritual blindness, pride. The writer speaks of a generation that is "pure in their own eyes", while, in reality, they are filthy before God. The result of pride is that they are deceived by it so that they cannot discover their real state before God. We sometimes euphemistically refer to this as a "blind spot".

Sadly, there are many leaders in the Body of Christ who are full of pride, yet remain blind to it. In leaders it often manifests in a refusal to work with others so that they become islands unto themselves. They feel no need for accountability or correction. They are not team players. They certainly don't understand God's plan to restore fathers and their need to be properly related to them. So they work alone and avoid any meaningful relationships, especially with those who are true apostolic fathers. While they may excel in natural leadership and ability, temporarily accomplishing wonderful things for God, they themselves never submit to counsel from others. They will steadfastly avoid any personal relationships where they might be exposed.

In their defense, it may be said that many of these leaders have been turned off by so-called apostolic leaders who have not exhibited a true "father's heart." The fleshly ambition seen in so many leaders today has left them with a bad taste in their mouth. Mention the word 'apostle' today and you can see apprehension appear on many faces. Many have been hurt by arbitrariness and legalism or by a hierarchical approach to apostolic leadership rather than a true, servant model. There are also those who want to build a financial pyramid for themselves. No wonder some find it difficult to trust true fathers who might really help them.

This is why leaders sometimes fall into sin. They are unable to see that they have not been "washed from the filthiness" in their own lives. There is no one who can admonish them. Because of this and their refusal to be related to true fathers they are missing out on the protection which God has provided in the church. True fathers are intended by God to save their sons from much grief. How sad to see sons repeating the sins and mistakes of their fathers because they are too self-sufficient or proud to listen and accept counsel.

At one time in his life, the apostle Peter was too proud and independent to accept what Jesus wanted to do in his life. On the eve of His Passion, when Jesus would wash both his feet and those of his other disciples , Peter protested vehemently and resisted:

"Peter said to Him, 'You shall never wash my feet!' Jesus answered him, If I do not wash you, you have no part with Me"   *(John 13:8)*

Behind Peter's refusal was not a humble heart too unworthy to accept what Jesus wanted to do. Rather, it was an independent heart that resisted! And the result was that Peter, at first, was unwilling to be washed by the Son of God. What a privilege he almost missed because of his pride and independence. Thankfully, the Lord worked patiently with his disciple until Peter was not only willing to have Jesus wash his feet, but his entire body as well.

What is important about this story is that Jesus extended this service to all of his people:

"If I then, your Lord and Teacher, have washed your feet, you also ought to wash one another's feet" (John 13:14).

69

Contrary to popular opinion the Lord was not instituting the sacrament of foot washing at this point. What He was doing was defining the ministry of the body of Christ as the service of "washing one another" in Christ. We must overcome that independence which is natural to all and learn to both wash others as well as receive the washing. Refusal to do so can only be attributed to our pride and independence—"I don't need anybody to wash my feet."

This has particular relevance to the relationship between apostolic fathers and sons in these last days. Apostles will have to overcome ambition and a desire to control others and learn to wash the feet of their sons in true humility and love. Sons, on the other hand, must learn to receive the washing in an attitude of true honor and respect (which in turn will wash the heart of fathers). God has so arranged this so that fathers need sons and sons need fathers?

To Receive, You Must Receive

John 1:12 states that only those who received Christ were able to become the sons of God. This of course is also true of apostolic counsel and input. In order to receive, you must do just that, receive! Even Jesus apparently was not able, (or didn't choose) to do wonders where they didn't receive him (Matt13:58). Many times I have witnessed a tremendous Holy Spirit impartation through a father just simply because he was received and honored as a father. It is amazing how the Holy Spirit can work through a relationship supernaturally when there is receptiveness.

Simple words and encouragement from a father have helped many a younger person in ministry. The only requirement was that he or she was willing to receive. A relationship if genuine, though small, is a vehicle within which the Holy Spirit may manifest. Many leave the ministry in discouragement because of not having such a relationship. It was the salvation of Israel and Egypt as well, that Pharaoh listened to the wise counsel of Joseph, whom God had made a father to Pharaoh (Gen 45:8).

The Rechabite Principle

If dishonoring fathers brings a curse upon us, the opposite is also true. Honoring them brings tremendous blessing! The Bible contains many wonderful statements regarding the blessing that flows to those who honor their fathers.

But perhaps the best example in Scripture is that of the story of the Rechabites in the Old Testament book of Jeremiah. Their story, found in Jeremiah, chapter thirty-five, is a wonderful example of how God blesses obedience.

Jeremiah was instructed by God to place a test before the sons of a man named Jonadab, the son of Rechab. The test was to place wine before them and ask them to drink with him. The Rechabites refused this invitation because their father, Jonadab, had previously given them a command not to drink wine, neither they nor their sons forever. The Rechabites would not violate the command of their father and therefore refused Jeremiah, remaining loyal to their pledge.

After the Rechabites refused the wine, the word of God came to Jeremiah. He was to make a comparison between the loyalty of the sons of Rechab to their father and the disloyalty of the sons of Judah to their Father. If the Rechabites continued to honor the word their father had spoken to them, how much more should the children of Israel honor the word of the living God? But they did not and therefore were ripe for judgment.

The thing we are to learn about the Rechabites is their absolute loyalty, honoring and obedience to their father; a loyalty that did not go unnoticed by God. God now speaks through Jeremiah that because of their honor and obedience to their father the Rechabites would not "want a man to stand before Him forever" (Jer. 35:19). What a fantastic promise! And all due to the fact that they honored their father's command and would not drink wine.

This is a powerful story that demonstrates how blessing is attached to honoring fathers—both earthly fathers as well as spiritual. In these days of restoration when God is raising up fathers in the Body of Christ we must learn to honor them properly if we want God to bless us as He did with the Rechabit

A Heart Problem

The same attitude of heart we have toward the heavenly Father is reflected by the attitude we have toward our earthly fathers. The writer of Hebrews seems to have understood this and makes it clear:

> *"Furthermore, we have had human fathers who corrected us,*
> *and we paid them respect. Shall we not much more readily be*
> *in subjection to the Father of spirits and live? For they*

> *indeed for a few days chastened us as seemed best to them,*
> *but He for our profit, that we may be partakers of His holi-*
> *ness" (Heb. 12:9-10).*

From God's comparison of the Rechabites with those who would not listen to the prophets, we may fairly draw the conclusion that dishonor or disobedience to an earthly father is a heart problem reflected by disobedience to God Himself. What the passage in Hebrews tells us is that disobedience brings a corresponding chastisement. Yet the flip side is equally true—obedience brings blessing. And if we are obedient to God it will be manifest by our honoring those who are fathers in our midst.

In the next chapter we will explore this further by looking at the life of a man who excelled in this matter of honoring fathers. It is possibly the reason that David was called a "man after God's own heart."

CHAPTER

14

WHY WAS DAVID BLESSED?

"Lord, my heart is not haughty, Nor my eyes lofty. Neither do I concern myself with great matters, Nor with things too profound for me." (Psalm 131:1)

In the entire Word of God (with the exception of Christ) there is no one who excels King David in the matter of having a right heart before God. He is God's benchmark of obedience and heart response for succeeding kings and leaders in Israel. In their obedience to God as well as their worship they were, for the most part, measured by the standard that their father David had set before them.

It is not difficult to understand the basis of David's success. He seems to have learned early what God had told the prophet Samuel when he was chosen from his brothers, that "God looks at the heart and not the outward appearance." David knew God's heart and God knew his. He learned early that blessing depended on his own heart attitude. David also learned early the importance of honoring fathers if he was to live in blessing and receive revelation from God.

A Story of Rejection

We should start by recognizing that David, like many of us, did not have a perfect father who raised him. The Bible doesn't say much about Jesse. Most of what we know about him is known primarily because of his relationship to his son. Yet we can read between the lines to understand a little of what David's early life was like.

After God had rejected Saul from being king, the prophet Samuel was instructed to go to Bethlehem and anoint a king from the sons of Jesse (I Samuel 16). He did not know which of Jesse's sons was God's choice. He was simply told to invite Jesse and his sons to a sacrifice and there, God would identify which of the young men he was to anoint.

At the feast Samuel reviewed each of Jesse's sons as they passed before him. Though each was impressive and Samuel was ready to anoint him, the Lord made it clear that He had rejected them. After all of the sons had passed before him Samuel inquired of Jesse, "Are all the young men here?" It was then that Jesse informed Samuel that there was one more son, David, who was tending the sheep and had not been invited to the feast. Samuel told Jesse that they would not sit down to eat until David was brought in. When David arrived, God instructed Samuel to anoint him as the future king of Israel and Samuel obeyed.

What is amazing is that Jesse had not even thought David important enough to invite to the feast either because he was the youngest or for some other reason. David must have felt some rejection at this point.

Apparently discord had been brewing in the family for some time, because, at a later date, David suffered even a greater rejection. When David's three brothers had gone to fight against Goliath with Saul's army, David was at home for a season looking after his father's sheep. His father sent him to visit his brothers at the battlefront to take some home delicacies to them and some cheese to their captain.

Upon arriving and delivering the provisions the giant Goliath came and uttered his threats against Israel. When David asked about the reward for killing Goliath, his brothers began to ridicule and humiliate him in front of everyone.

> *"Now Eliab his oldest brother heard when he spoke to the men; and Eliab's anger was aroused against David, and he said, 'Why did you come down here? And with whom have you left those few sheep in the wilderness? I know your pride and the insolence of your heart, for you have come down to see the battle.' And David said, 'What have I done now? Is there not a cause?' Then he turned from him toward another and said the same thing; and these people answered him as the first ones did"* (I Samuel 17:28-30).

This attitude of derision of David's brothers towards him at that time certainly did not occur overnight, but was obviously an extension of their previous feelings about him. His brothers put him down just as his father had discounted him when Samuel came to pick a king. They unjustly accused him of pride,

I have observed how many times the older children in a family will pick on the youngest. Often he or she will be "put in a box", so to speak, and never get out of it in the eyes of the elders. It is often hard for those who know us intimately to perceive God working maturity and perfection in us. Rather do they judge us according to the past and reject us. We can not grow up in their eyes. It is tragic when this type of attitude operates in a family or a church, when those who are mature cannot release the babes to come further in God. The true worth of the person is thereby rejected.

In the midst of it all **there is no bible record of David ever having an improper heart attitude towards his father or brothers**. He was a perfectly obedient son, taking cheese and raisins to his brothers at the battle when he was told. And in the midst of his brothers' rejection at the battlefront he refused to wallow in self-pity letting it cast a pall over his life and ministry. Rather, he kept his mind and spirit clear. Thus he could accurately hear God and was able to take the opportunity to kill Goliath and win a great victory for the Lord and Israel. It is safe to say that David could not have fulfilled God's purpose for him at that moment had he been full of self-pity and offense. A friend of mine once said, " There is a lot of rejection and condemnation in the world, but I have made up my mind not to receive any of it." To understand our true worth to God is a great help in such stressful situations.

Rejection by a Spiritual Father

David was later adopted into Saul's household and called to serve the king. It wasn't long before more rejection came to test him. This time, it came from a spiritual father. David's obvious anointing in warfare and leadership brought down the wrath of an insecure Saul. Prompted by an evil spirit, Saul would spend many years persecuting David, actually attempting to take his life on several occasions. Though many today complain about their father's treatment of them, how many have had a powerful warrior-king like Saul hurl a javelin at them and attempt to pin them to the wall? (I Sam 19:10). At least twice in David's life this happened to him.

On at least two occasions, David had opportunity to actually rid himself of Saul but refused, though his men urged him. On one of these occasions (I Samuel 24::3-20) there is a beautiful story which demonstrates David's heart towards Saul. In tender terms, David refers to Saul as "his father" (vs. 11), while Saul refers to him as "his son" (vs. 16). So right was David's heart towards his spiritual father that he was smitten in conscience for even cutting off Saul's robe. The robe of the king represented his station (reputation) in life and David was broken for violating that reputation in any way, even the cutting off of a small piece. How wonderful if the Body of Christ would be as sensitive in treating those whom God anoints! How often, while avoiding an overt attack of others we will still insinuate certain small things about a person in order to undermine his or her position. We cut off a piece of his robe! David grieved, having done that. He would allow no root of bitterness to spring up in his heart, even though being severely rejected. Regardless of Saul's behavior he was a spiritual father and David behaved himself properly towards him before God. It is interesting to note that David's reward for his behavior was to receive a prophetic statement from Saul himself that he would not only prosper, but would be king one day (v. 20).

How Sweet It Is !

Twice in my life I have had the experience of receiving encouraging prophecy from someone who was in total opposition to me at the time. My favorite memory of this comes from the day I was set in as a pastor some thirty-five odd years ago. A truly prophetic yet undisciplined gentleman who had continually caused spiritual havoc in the church, popped in half way through the ordination meeting that Sunday and took a seat in the back of the hall. I had just solidly rebuked him several days before for certain unruly behavior and asked him to refrain from prophesying for a season. He had left very upset with me, stating that he would not be back. And there he was. I prayed silently that God would not let him open his mouth, for I felt he meant me no good. Suddenly he stood up and in a booming voice began one of the most encouraging prophecies concerning my future that I ever was privileged to receive. That prophecy has meant much over the years as various battles have come. I knew that that prophecy had to be from God, for I am sure that the brother would not have originated it in his own heart. I have fought a good warfare sustained by that prophecy on many occasions.

I can only imaging that David hung onto the prophecy delivered by Saul in 1 Sam 24:20. I can see in my mind's eye David huddled in his cloak on many a dark night, meditating on and savoring that word from God in his heart.

David Honors Saul

For refusing to take matters in his own hands, God honored David. He was finally delivered from Saul. David shines even more after Saul's death than when Saul was alive. Who would have blamed David for rejoicing at the news of Saul's death? Yet David continued to afford Saul the honor he had bestowed on him when he was alive. You see, it was in David's heart to honor a father on principle, not because of his perceived worthiness, or for political reasons.

When Saul died on the mountains of Gilboa it was the men of Jabesh-Gilead that retrieved Saul's and Jonathan's bodies from the wall at Bethshan and gave them a proper burial. This was in response to the fact that during his lifetime Saul had rallied Israel's army and defended the men of Jabesh-Gilead when they were being attacked.[1] One of the first acts of David after becoming king was to commend the men of Jabesh-Gilead for honoring Saul.

David would have been justified in our eyes for trying to wipe out the memory of Saul and consolidate his own position. Abner, Saul's former commander, was already attempting to garner support to overthrow David. Yet David understood the principle of honoring a father, even though he had been so badly mistreated by him during his life. In New Testament terms he knew the truth of giving

---

1 This is a wonderful story which indicates the immeasurable value of the vertical relationship (See Chapter 22 for a discussion of vertical relationships) which can bring deliverance in a time of need. The men of Jabesh were in dire straits and asked the newly appointed King to help them. The story is found in 1 Samuel 11:1-11 and should be read thoroughly at this point.

"honor to whom honor is due" (Romans 13:7). The honor was because he was God's anointed, not because he was a man or king only. This was a fundamental rule of life to David and one that would bring him life, success and prosperity.

Upon Saul's death, David publicly lamented with fasting and weeping (2 Samuel 1). He even wrote a beautiful song about this including Jonathan in his grief. He also had Saul's Amalekite slayer put to death in a display of genuine grief and horror at the young man's lack of respect for God's anointed authority. David then sent for Saul's bones and brought them up to be buried with great honor in Saul's family sepulcher. David continued to honor Saul for many years after his death. He knew the commandment to "honor your father and mother" and received the blessing that accompanies it.

Honoring Fathers Today

The example of David is a powerful model for young men today. There are many who have been temporarily placed in situations where they are subjected to men like Saul, men who do not have their best interests at heart. We have heard the horror stories over the years of how those in authority have spiritually abused those under them in the name of submission. While such abuse is never justified, God often uses such situations to teach young men and women how to honor fathers regardless of their treatment of them. We must settle this principle in our hearts that to honor fathers is to honor God. When we find ourselves in such a circumstance, God has not abandoned us, but has much to teach us during the situation. As always the question is not "have we been wronged", but "how are we choosing to respond?"

Unfortunately, there are many that fail this test and despise those fathers in their life. They are embittered or at the least lightly esteem them. They can only talk about the abuse or neglect they suffered at their hands and therefore dishonor them. In the least they cut off their robes verbally, at the worst they attempt to kill them with their words. How easily David could have succumbed to that spirit and ended up despising and dishonoring Saul. I am sure that he could have found many in Israel that would have commiserated with his bitterness. Yet the "man after God's own heart" rose above it and honored Saul long after he was gone. He knew the truth that God honored fathers and practiced it in his own life.

Fear of God, the Key

Of course, at the heart of David's willingness to honor Saul was a healthy fear of God. It is unlikely that we will give honor to fathers, especially those who wrong and misuse us, if we do not have that respect for God that transforms all human relationships. This is what made David the "man after God's own heart." And it is that alone that will allow us to give proper honor to those whom God has put in our life, even if they have not acted with our best interest at heart. Our daily prayer should be Ps 51:10 "Create in me a clean heart, O God; and renew a right spirit within me."

PART THREE:

PROBLEMS WE GENERATE

CHAPTER

15

HONORING SONS

"My son, give me your heart, And let your eyes observe my ways." (Prov 23: 26)

We have seen that God expects sons and daughters to give proper honor to natural and spiritual fathers. Not only is this a clearly stated principle of God's word, it is intended to be the means of great blessing in our lives. Life, blessing, revelation, and prosperity all flow from such obedience. To their credit there have been many young men who have behaved properly towards spiritual fathers and have been greatly blessed in the process.

That being said, how much better it would be if apostles and other church governmental leaders, unlike Saul, behaved in such a way that the sons would have no difficulty honoring and submitting to them. In this section of the book we want to look at the problems generated by many would be apostles. How do they make it difficult for sons and daughters to relate properly? We have already looked at those godly heart traits that an apostle should demonstrate. We will now see some problems and also some godly behavior that would alleviate much of the strain between fathers and sons. It should become obvious that as fathers embody these traits in their lives they make it easy for sons to honor them. Blessing will flow automatically from above. Conversely, if some of the things I am about to point out exist in a leader's life, then he will always see turmoil and hurt and lack of life and anointing. It is not God's best for sons and daughters to have to honor or submit to fathers "in spite of how they act", but rather because of it.

Saulish Leaders

One of the problems among leaders in the Body of Christ today is that many of them have mistakenly drawn their concept of who leaders are and how they function from the world. There, leaders are viewed as those sitting on the top of the heap, the ones with all of the authority who get to boss the others around. They equate leadership with charisma, position and authority.

We have seen in the previous chapter that this was the concept of leadership held by Israel's first king. Saul, who had no fear of or faith in God, believed that he had to maintain his authority from whoever assaulted it, real or perceived. He had forgotten that it was God who had given him his position and authority in Israel. He had forgotten that it was God Who preserved him in that authority. Having lost connection to God, he embarked on a crusade to protect his throne from any would-be usurper. This led to deception and paranoia. Perceiving wrongly that David was trying to take his throne, he spent the remaining years of his life trying to kill the one that God had sent to help him. Sauls do not recognize their enablers, but fear them. Davids honor and esteem their mighty men and make room for them!

There are Saulish leaders in the Church today. They live their lives in the fear and insecurity that someone might steal their ministry or take their authority. This has devastating results if such a person is a pastor of a church. Often such a leader will resort to manipulation and other soulish tactics to get people to do what he wants to do. It is all justified in the name of "saving the church" or "protecting the sheep", but it really has to do with a man "protecting his turf."

The results are even more hurtful in the case of apostles who have authority or influence over many churches. I have personally witnessed the abuse that has occurred when men claiming apostolic authority have sought to direct the affaris of local churches with little or no regard for local authority. Local authority also comes from God. Wielding apostolic authority can be heady stuff to some and when those yielding it take their cue from worldly or secular models the result is devastated lives and an eventual weakening of the root of real authority.

What is the problem with such leaders? True apostles are those who understand that real authority is always delegated to them from Jesus Christ Himself! The problem is not with the notion that such men should have authority—it is that such authority is being wielded by those who lack the essential understanding, maturity and developed character traits for leadership in the Body of Christ. For the fact remains, anointed leaders in the Body of Christ are those who exercise authority properly through a Christ-like character and through a relationship with those whom they govern. The idea that oversight means authority, without deep and meaningful relationships, integrity and good character is false.

This must be understood if we are going to see true father apostles emerge on the scene today. They must be those who speak and act with authority, yet without a "control" atmosphere constantly about them. Such men can exercise real authority because in their character they exhibit the nature of the Lamb. And like the Lamb they must demonstrate the "meekness and gentleness" which are in Christ.

CHAPTER

16

MEEKNESS AND GENTLENESS

"Everyone proud in heart is an abomination to the Lord;
Though they join forces, none will go unpunished."
(Prov 16:5)

Go to a leadership seminar or ask most people today what are the most important characteristics of true leadership and you will rarely, if ever, find meekness and gentleness on the agenda. God's ideas of the most important qualifications for leaders are often very different from ours. That becomes even more apparent when we realize how God views meekness and gentleness. In the world, this quality is never associated with leadership. Yet in the kingdom it is an indispensable quality for those who would lead men, especially those who are apostolic fathers in the faith.

We can look at both the Old and New Testaments to find numerous examples of this quality in God's people. We have already seen how David is a role model for how sons should relate to fathers. David is further an excellent example of a leader. David himself excelled in this quality of meekness and gentleness. How did he learn the importance of this quality? By seeing that it was the way in which God Himself had dealt with him:

> *"You have also given me the shield of Your salvation; your right hand has held me up, your gentleness has made me great. You enlarged my path under me; so my feet did not slip. I have pursued my enemies and overtaken them; neither did I turn back again till they were destroyed. I have wounded them, so that they could not rise; they have fallen under my feet"(Psalm 18:35-38).*

David acknowledges that his heavenly Father had made him great even in the violent pursuit of warfare. This scripture makes it clear that the molding factor in his success was gentleness—God's gentleness had a deep effect on him. What a statement! David said that it was God's very humility, his 'stooping down' to help him that made him successful in what he did. This should put to rest forever the notion that gentleness is to be associated with weak leadership.

Lovingkindness is Better than Life

Once there was a man who had a teenage son who was just like him in temperament. Both father and son had strong personalities. They loved each other very much, but the inevitable clashes began to come as the boy sought to establish his own identity and emerge into manhood.

The father had pushed very hard for many years in building his own life and ministry, and in doing so had not really done a good job in securing the relationship with his son. This coupled with the natural insensitivity of his personality caused a growing problem. A push on the part of the son to establish his own ground developed slowly into a rebellious attitude, because the father didn't take kindly to the slightest opposition. He wasn't used to "subordinates" speaking up to him. This son, cut out of the same mold, stood up more and more. One day he stood eyeball to eyeball, in fact slightly taller than his father, and refused to obey a direct order. In a flash of revelation, the father suddenly realized that he was powerless to do anything about this immediate situation, short of a fistfight. He was pretty sure he couldn't win that. Ten years earlier he would have removed his belt, and the whole thing would have been solved.

He turned and slowly walked away, partly in sadness, partly in stunned anger, but also with a hollow feeling that somehow he had just lost some authority. He began to talk seriously with the Lord about this son. Instead of receiving a new revelation on how to lead, he was surprised to hear the Lord say, "Loving kindness is better than life, just love him instead of commanding him and see what happens."

The father loved this son very deeply and was truly disturbed by the turn of events. He began to totally reverse his tactics. With Christ's help a leopard can change his spots. There would be no more authoritative manner, just love and acceptance. Fishing trips with genuine fellowship ensued. There was an attempt to treat the son with respect and as though he were the adult which he was rapidly becoming.

A few months later, in January, the two were on a deep-sea fishing trip in the Florida Keys. The father had been sick for some time, but was recuperating. Suddenly at night the temperature dropped way down, one of those freak times that can hit in Florida. The place they were staying had no heat and the windows were not designed to retain any. About three o'clock in the morning, the father was dimly aware that someone was hovering over his bed in the dark. It was the son, who had gotten up, gone to the car parked about a block away, obtained a car robe, and was now placing it gently over the father. Realizing he had wakened the older man, the son said, "I love you, Dad. I didn't want you to get cold." The father's heart surged with gratitude and was warmed more than his body. The Lord's counsel had been so good.

As time went by, the father discovered that his real authority had never diminished. In fact, it had grown. The son readily came to him for counsel out of respect and desire. A tremendous relationship developed which allowed the father to truly "cover" his son while he was achieving manhood and his own sense of wholesome independence. Gentleness truly makes one great and loving kindness truly is better than life.

When we come to the New Testament none excels in this quality more than the great apostle to the Gentiles. Some erroneously perceive Paul to have been a very obstinate man with whom it was difficult to get along. It is true that he was a man of great resolve who would not be deterred from accomplishing his mission.

Yet that does not mean that he was difficult in his dealings with God's people. The truth is, he was the very epitome of gentleness when dealing with those who were called in Christ as he himself reminded the Thessalonians:

> *"But we were gentle among you, just as a nursing mother*
> *cherishes her own children. So, affectionately longing for*
> *you, we were well-pleased to impart to you not only the gos-*
> *pel of God, but also our own lives, because you had become*
> *dear to us" (I Thessalonians 2:7-8)).*

How rarely we think of Paul in this manner. It is true that Paul was a man of great faith and courage, a stickler for maintaining the truth, and he was certainly not a wimp. Yet he regards himself as a nursemaid towards his own spiritual children, willing to lay down his own life to supply what they needed. For Paul, this is one of the main evidences of his apostolic credentials. Remember that gentleness is, after all, a fruit of the Holy Spirit.

Sadly, this quality is often pretty much lacking in those who are considered apostolic leaders today. I have seen those in apostolic oversight, when they can't turn a church problem around quickly enough to suit them, arbitrarily sell off buildings, fire pastors without scriptural or ethical reasons and put their own people in place. They make pronouncements and decisions without fully investigating and knowing the mind of the Lord. Sadly due to their lack of gentleness and patience, such men have left many devastated lives in their wake and many potential leaders are shipwrecked.

It is obvious that both David and Paul reflected the leadership model of Jesus in their own lives. Paul seems to have understood this when addressing the Corinthians:

> *"Now I Paul, myself am pleading with you by the **meekness***
> ***and gentleness of Christ**—who in presence am lowly among*
> *you, but being absent am bold toward you" (II Cor. 10:1)*

Even Jesus during His earthly life spoke of this quality as that which would appeal to his hearers and bid them to come (Matthew 11:28-29). The importance of this quality cannot be underestimated, especially since the Lord cites it as his chief characteristic inducing men to follow Him. And once we realize how important it is that this quality is seen in our lives, all the more in those who are apostles, the more effective we will become. It may not be overemphasizing it to say that apostles above all else, must be those who excel in gentleness and meekness.

17

THE GRACE OF BEING TEACHABLE

"The heart of the prudent acquires knowledge, And the ear of the wise seeks knowledge." (Prov 18:15)

While it is easy to cite much scripture asserting the importance of this quality it is not as easy to define it. One word above all expresses in a practical way what is at the heart of gentleness and meekness. It is the word teachable. When we experience meekness and gentleness it will show up as our willingness to receive from others. This is even more important for leaders, especially those who would be fathers in the faith.

This goes to the heart of our concept of leadership. Far too many leaders have the idea that real leadership is the ability to boss others around and remain at the top of the pecking order. They have no real compunction to receive from those they consider to be underlings. It comes down to the fact that a worldly concept of leadership is embraced, one that Jesus spoke against as typifying the Gentiles of his day:

*"But Jesus called them to Himself and said, "You know that the rulers of the Gentiles **lord it over** them, and those who are great exercise authority over them. Yet it shall not be so among you; but whoever desires to become great among you, let him be your servant. And whoever desires to be first among you, let him be your slave." (Matt: 20:25-27)*

This attitude was not to characterize those of His kingdom. Rather than being perceived as those at the top, Jesus insisted that true leaders in the kingdom consider themselves at the bottom of the heap—the ones who get to serve everyone else! This also means a willingness to listen to anyone without discounting him or her.

Moses had a Blind Spot, Do I?

This grace to be teachable is critical to the success of any leader. It is not an exaggeration to say that Moses, as great a leader as he was, would not have succeeded if it wasn't for the fact that he could receive correction from his father-in-law who wisely discerned that he was counseling too much. (Exodus 17:13-27) How is it that the man who met God face to face on the mount could not see that he was taxing both himself and the people by his actions? The simple answer is that even the best leaders have blind spots—those areas where they are unable to see themselves as others do. While God may choose to speak to them directly, he often will use others. If we cannot receive from others then we are putting ourselves in the place of refusing help from God. To Moses' credit he was not only teachable but could receive from his father-in-law This is one reason why the Holy Spirit says that he was the meekest man upon the earth (Num 12:3).

The Lord does not Guide the Proud

It is absolutely necessary that apostles exhibit this quality in their lives. They must be willing to receive from others and that means even a rebuke when necessary. The scripture again seems to present David as a perfect example of this trait. When Nathan the prophet rebuked him for his adultery and murder

(II Samuel 11), David not only received the rebuke, but deeply humbled himself before the Lord. Later, David would write these great words found in Psalm 25:4-5,9:

> *"Show me Your ways, O Lord; **teach me Your paths**. Lead me in your truth and teach me, for You are the God of my salvation; on You I wait all the day. The **humble He guides** in justice, and the **humble He teaches** His way"(emphasis added)*

Another powerful story of the importance of being teachable is found in the story of the healing of Namaan in Second Kings, chapter five. Namaan, commander of the Syrian army, was a leper. A captive Jewish maiden who was a servant to Namaan's wife told her about a prophet in Samaria who could heal her husband. With permission from his king, Namaan went to the prophet Elisha who told him what was required for his healing. He was to wash himself "seven times in the Jordan River. (2 Kings 5:10) Yet upon hearing this Namaan was doubly offended. For one thing, the prophet himself never even came out to see him but rather, sent a servant to deliver the message. For another, Namaan was instructed to wash himself in the Jordan, an ignoble river compared to the great rivers of Syria. With his pride wounded, Namaan turned away in a rage and rebelled against the word of the prophet, and thus the Word of God.

Another servant of Namaan's reasoned with him and Namaan reluctantly obeyed the prophet's word and was healed. The result was not only the restoration of his flesh, but a revelation that the God of Israel was the true and living God whom He would now worship (5:15-19)

Twice the Lord used subordinates to speak the truth to this powerful and proud man. In his pride, Namaan could not see that God was speaking to him through those he considered insignificant or who had offended him. When we are proud and unteachable we will always miss those times when God is speaking to us. God very often does have something to say through the very least of the brethren if we are able to hear it. The problem is, we often manifest a subtle elitism in which we refuse to humble ourselves and listen to others, especially those whom we consider subordinate.

Honoring the Sons

Since God can speak at any time through anyone, it is extremely important to esteem those around us by being teachable. This sets the stage for them to come and help us. Perhaps the apostle Paul summed it up best when he told the church at Rome:

> *"Who are you to judge another man's servant? To his own master he stands or falls. Indeed, he will be made to stand, for God is able to make him stand."(Rom 14:4)*

Anyone who is born again and is baptized into the Body of Christ is technically a servant of Christ and has immeasurable worth and value. Therefore, when we demean anyone in the church in our heart we are offending the Lord, who is both his Master and ours. And those we demean, especially the younger person or peer can always sense when they are being disregarded.

Apostles must be those who esteem and honor their sons thus making it easier for them to receive. This is the spirit that Paul seems to have moved in when he was among the churches he founded. While he makes it clear that he could have come and exercised his authority as an apostle, he chose rather to come in a humble spirit honoring those he moved among.

Elitism is Alive and Well Today

Unfortunately, there is often a spirit of elitism today among those claiming to be apostles which is the very opposite of the way that Paul walked. "I am an apostle and therefore I know more than you. Because of my anointing, I am somewhat infallible. Sit down and let me tell you what you need to know." While few would ever give voice to such a thought in public it often exists in their hearts and controls their actions. It places higher value on position than it does on relationship.

Several times in my life I have been involved in oversight situations in local churches where there has been a struggle for control. As such I have had to deal with men from outside who were trying to affect the local situation. They were trying to get in "through a side door" or "over a wall" as it were, and had no real regard for the existing, established authority that was in place. Often they were simply trying to usurp authority (about which we will speak later). They seemed to believe that their perceived position in the Kingdom was such that it gave them the right to overstep local authority.

What impression do young sons get when they see spiritual fathers disregarding authority? It always breeds confusion and usually leaves many hurting people in its wake. It also raises up sons who in their own time have little regard for authority. A role model is a powerful thing!

Rebellion Feeds on Supposed Authority

At any time when division arises in a church, there is usually a rebellious faction of people involved. Rebellion feeds on some kind of perceived authority, even if that authority is spurious. The enemy will always see to it that the rebellious ones gravitate to any perceived outside authority that is questioning the real, God-established authority. The times I have witnessed this happen I am convinced that the invaders meant no malice. Their ambition and desire for greater territory was simply leading them to try to move the landmarks of authority. They imagined that their calling and position put them somehow above God's order. This is a form of lawlessness, about which I shall mention later. That is always a pathway to trouble and further confusion. It is a manifestation of elitism. It is not teachable.

Such an attitude sets men and women at naught, especially the younger and lesser. Yet such a way is not the way of a true apostle in the kingdom. Paul was Timothy's father in the faith, but he demonstrated none of this elitism in his heart. He exhorted all of the churches to fully receive his young son and commanded them to respect him and not despise his youth.

Paul considered himself as the "least of the apostles". This is remarkable! As the least he did not need to continually protect his reputation or make sure that all of the churches looked only to him, but could push them toward Timothy. It is only when you see yourself as 'great' that you feel a need to protect that greatness. The Kingdom of Christ loomed larger to Paul than personal recognition. This is one of the main spiritual gifts of an apostle; to be able to see the treasure hidden in the earthen vessels. To push forward sons who are leaders of the future. This gift will not operate where there is elitism.

Elitism tends to make one overlook the potential God has placed in others. It looks for whatever can serve and elevate itself rather than what will serve and elevate the Kingdom of Christ. It will discount the gifts and anointing God has placed in the Body. It is not teachable and is usually very critical of others. Scripture is clear that God hates this attitude (Proverbs 6:16-17).

CHAPTER

18

DEVILISH AMBITION

"There are many plans in a man's heart, Nevertheless the Lord's counsel--that will stand." (Prov 19:21)

"And do you seek great things for yourself? Do not seek them; for behold, I will bring adversity on all flesh, says the Lord." (Jer 45:5)

History books as well as the Holy Bible reveal that much murder and violence have occurred as a result of ambition. Young kings upon coming to the throne have murdered their siblings to consolidate their positions. Sons have dispatched fathers, as in the case of the Assyrian King, Sennacherib. (2 Chron 32:21) There is something evil in the hearts of many men that causes jealousy to arise when a sense of competition sets in. It started with Cain. It is satanic in origin.

There is a noted fable that somewhat illustrates this phenomenon. As the account goes, " the devil was crossing the desert in Libya when he came upon a group of lesser demons who were tempting a holy hermit. They tried him with seductions of the flesh; they sought to sour his mind with doubts and fears; they told him that all his austerities were worth nothing. But nothing worked; the holy man was impeccable. Then the devil stepped forward and addressing the imps, he said, 'Your methods are too crude. Permit me for one moment. This is what I should recommend'. Going up to the hermit, he said, ' Have you heard the news? Your brother has been made the Bishop of Alexandria'. The fable says that jealousy began to cloud the serene face of the holy man."

While this story amply illustrates the devilish effects of carnal ambition it needs to be said that not all ambition is of the demonic or fleshly kind. In fact, Scripture commends a certain type of ambition that might well be called "kingdom ambition." For instance, the apostle Paul makes it clear that having a desire to be a overseer in the church is a good and worthy ambition (I Timothy 3:1). In fact, such a desire is a prerequisite to holding the office and must be evident if the person is to be considered. We need to clearly separate kingdom ambition from self-ambition.

The question that must always be asked is, "Where is our ambition aimed? Is it for Christ and His kingdom or is it for our own personal advancement?" Great honesty and soul searching on one's knees before the Lord is required before answering. Human or self-ambition is clearly Satanic in origin having its roots in Satan's own self-promotion. It is traditionally believed that it is Satan speaking in the fourteenth chapter of Isaiah where he promotes himself above the very throne of God. (14:13-14) This self-aggrandizement has at its core the desire to have the attention and worship due only to God. And it was this ambition that apparently turned a beautiful seraph into the prince of evil, the sworn enemy of God and his purpose in the universe.

In this chapter, I want to expose devilish ambition for what it is. This is critical in regards to those who would be apostles. They must be those who, like the Lord Jesus, have no ambition except to see the Kingdom of God extended, exalted and to see their children fulfill their destinies in Christ.

Wrong Ambition

It is true that God so constructed us as to desire the love and friendship of others. It is only when that desire for approval is placed above the approval of God that what is good becomes sinful. It is a sad fact that many leaders today seem to find their own identity by seeking the approval of others. This, in turn, often leads to wrong ambition. A few men have built their entire ministries on such ambition.

It is not difficult to detect wrong ambition, especially in leaders since it is easily detected by the actions that it inspires. It has a stink of its own. It often exhibits a controlling spirit. The Bible states that witchcraft is resident in the flesh (Galatians 5:20). Before witchcraft produces its demonic fruit it has to work through the flesh. Those moving in ambition only look to manipulate people and use them for their own purpose and end. They look to take authority when they can get away with it and are unable to submit to others. They are not team players.

Ambition is also manifested in a tendency to constantly put down other people and their ideas if it feels itself threatened by them. It puts others in boxes, categorizes them, and files them away never to rise above a certain level in the eyes of the leader. Those leaders moving in personal ambition usually view people as stepping stones, only having worth in regards to their own plans.

There is a passage in 1 Samuel 14:52 that gives us a small glimpse into ambition as it applies to building in one's own strength. "...When Saul saw any strong man or any valiant man, he took him for himself". Compare this to David's attitude toward God. David allowed the Holy Spirit to send him future men of valor to the cave of Adullam and also thereafter at Ziklag and Hebron. David was content to let the Lord build the house. If our heart is right and God is behind what we are doing, He will send everyone we need to do the work. We don't have to buy people 's strength or otherwise strive to attract their ability. God will create the relationships if we are obedient. Note that many of the mighty men God gave him were not all that attractive at the start (1 Sam 22:2).

If an ambitious leader is in the presence of the real anointing or a person with a more agile and understanding mind than his own, he will often feel the need to put that person down. Sadly, such a leader cannot bear for someone to surpass him in excellence or achievement (unless he can give the impression that he had something to do with their success). Real apostles, as we have seen, rejoice when their sons surpass them. While we have seen men give lip service to this idea from the pulpit, in action and deed they continue to vie for preeminence, thus quenching the development of those around them.

Ambition imagines vacuums in leadership situations. It mistakes patience and "waiting on the Lord" for a lack of initiative. It is insensitive and will dive right into situations and attempt to fill the imagined vacuum with its own presumptive leadership. It generally sees position as being greater than relationship and will strive for position. If it thinks it sees a vacuum, it will usurp authority to fill it if it can.

Ambitious Apostles

In the last thirty years a flurry of apostolic movements has arisen, led in general by men of God, full of fire and zeal. For the most part this has been God's initiative. He is restoring the truth of fivefold ministry teams and apostolic-prophetic building teams. This has been a welcome development since Ephesians 4:11-12 is crucial to understanding the building and equipping of the church. Unfortunately while many have been able to clearly articulate the concept, there has been little of the practical working out of this in reality. In fact, many that have touted the restoration of the five-fold ministry have often exhibited the most carnal ambition. Many could teach marketing techniques on Madison Avenue. When men are marketing their networks instead of the Kingdom of God and the purposes of Christ, it is usually pretty obvious to Christian observer who is serious about the matters discussed in this book. Paul said it was proper to "persuade men", but only about the things of Christ.

Ambition Draws Ambition as Deep Calls unto Deep

In some apostolic networks young men will follow an ambitious leader because they have nowhere else to go and because there is often an exciting marketing and an articulate vision accompanying the movement. Other young men will follow because of their own ambitious drive. While they may discern the presence of worldly ambition in the leader, they are hoping that by associating with him they will be rewarded for their loyalty and eventually advanced. We have seen men jump on the bandwagon of an apostolic movement in a similar way that people get involved with political movements. Learning the art of politics they are hoping that their "hour in the sun" might come some day and they will then have the opportunity to control others. So they vie for the favor of the leader in the hopes of being promoted. It is common to hear statements like "moving up in the ministry" and "a higher level of ministry" and "we are on the cutting edge".

As in political parties, this eventually gives rise to an inevitable "pecking order" where those who are the most skilled in the art of politics and are willing to perform for the leader are brought into the inner circle. These networks are performance oriented. This inevitably breeds favoritism. Those in the inner circle are exalted. Very often discouragement and discontent begins to form in the "lower ranks" as certain brethren are overlooked. Those who are not personally ambitious but are content to quietly wait upon the Lord are often perceived as being too laid back, passive, or lacking in motivation. Sadly, they are often perceived as being lacking in leadership ability and are passed over.

What is the problem in such movements? For one, they thrive on performance much as a secular business does. This not to say that performance is unimportant. Performance must be done "unto the Lord" and for the sake of the vision, not unto the leader with a view of getting a leg up on the ladder. For another, they often judge men by their charisma and achievement, rather than their character and the fruit of the Spirit. A wise man of God once said that, "what a man builds with his gift he often destroys with his character." When we are willing to overlook obvious character flaws for the sake of the "work" and the "vision" we are headed for trouble. It is wise to remember that Satan never attacks a man or woman in his or her gift. He always attacks the character.

"Bear" Bryant

Several years ago I was at an alumni meeting in Selma, Alabama, at the time when Coach Paul "Bear" Bryant had just taken over the University of Alabama football program. The "Bear" began to tell us what he expected to accomplish and how he would do it. He began at one point to talk about the kind of young men he would recruit. He made a statement I will never forget. He said, "Some of you think that football builds character. Well, I'll tell you right now that I don't plan to waste my time trying to teach character. I want the young men that come into my program to already have good character. I'll teach them how to play football." In the church, we will have compassion on those who have flaws in their character and do all that we can to help them change. We will not reject them from fellowship. But no matter how gifted they are, there is no excuse for overlooking serious character flaws just to get a person's gift involved in the ministry. When it comes to government in the church, it is doubly true.

CHAPTER

19

MOVING LANDMARKS

"He who has a deceitful heart finds no good" (Prov 17:20)

One day, while reading in my Bible, Deuteronomy 27:17 jumped off the page:

"Cursed is the one who moves his neighbor's landmark."

I had preached on the subject of landmarks and had listened to others do so many times. Mostly what I had heard pertained to keeping doctrine pure. But that day I saw something new.

A landmark in ancient Israel defined one's inheritance. When Jabez asked God to increase his borders or inheritance in 1 Chr 4:10, the word in Hebrew refers to landmarks. Landmarks delineate an inheritance. They proscribe a piece of land. He was asking God to increase his inheritance. David said, "the lines have fallen to me in pleasant places" in Ps 16:6, and concludes the verse with a declaration that he indeed had a good inheritance. In stretching the lines to measure and describe an inheritance, they are always stretched from landmark to landmark. As an attorney in my younger days in Alabama, I often used land-marks to describe a tract of land in a deed.

As you and I have built churches, authority, relationships, won converts, and the like; these things have become part of our Kingdom inheritance as individu-als. I gave twenty-two years of my life and energy to the building of a church. What was done through me by the Spirit of God is part of my inheritance. Please don't misunderstand. I know well that the church belongs to Jesus Christ and not to me. We are, however, co-heirs with Christ. According to 2 Cor 5:10, we will receive a good or bad inheritance on judgment day, depending upon our earthly walk.

Now, just like brother Jabez, (1 Chron 4:9-10) I have spent my later years asking God for a greater spiritual inheritance, and working at gaining it. I have tried so far as I know, to work legally.

As a young lawyer in the rural south in my earlier days, I saw how an unscru-pulous lawyer could use deception, the law and the ignorance of people to dupe unsuspecting heirs out of their rightful estates. Sometimes this was done using the technicalities of the law. World history is basically a story of men, tribes and nations taking land from each other.

If you have been in the ministry for very long and have built anything of substance for the Lord, you are aware that there are brethren who will try to move your landmarks and take part of your inheritance if they can. They did it to Paul the apostle, and they do it today. Ambitious men are still around. They will attempt to lure talented brethren into their camps.

When I first had this thought, I fell to my knees and cried out to God. Had I ever moved anyone's landmarks? I want to be blessed. I wanted the hand of God to be with me. When others had tried to move my landmarks and take part of my inheritance, I had gotten angry and incensed. Was I perhaps reaping what I had sown? The Holy Spirit was gracious and pointed out that there were times when I had been guilty. I was young in the ministry and didn't understand what I understand now, but nevertheless I was guilty. I repented with all my heart. I told the Lord that if there were any way possible to go back and undo what I had done, I would do it. I meant it! But spilled water cannot be picked up. Like Jabez, I ask God daily to keep me from evil and sinning in this way ever again. I do not want to be a source of pain to any brother or sister if I can help it.

CHAPTER 19

You see, we apostles need to be sowing blessing and not filling the field with curses. Wrong ambition will cause you to try to move in on another man's inheritance. Paul, our role model, did not wish to build on another's foundation.

Two Legal Ways to Increase Your Inheritance

There are only two legitimate ways to increase your sphere of influence and authority, your inheritance! The first is to do what Jabez did. Ask God to increase your borders. He will gladly do this if your heart motives are right. He will do it by divine encounters, by sending people to you, by giving you revelation, and yes, even by increasing finances. Isaiah 9:7 tells us that there will be no end to the increase of the Lord's government. There is enough authority and territory for everyone that wants it legally. We don't ever have to move anyone else's landmarks. The apostle Paul made it quite clear in Rom 15:20 that he had no desire to build on another man's foundation.

The Pie is Huge

Picture for a moment the inheritance as a huge pie. The Lord is at the center. It is His pie. Each slice increases in width as it radiates out from the Lord. The pie is infinite. My slice, although tiny at the point of starting, increases dramatically as I continue outward toward where the crust would be. So does yours. My slice can become as large as I have faith and energy to make it as I simply obey the Lord. Yours too. There is never a need or a reason for me to have to take any of your pie.

The second way to increase an inheritance legally is by marriage. This speaks of a new relationship where two inheritances are combined, neither party losing anything, but both gaining what the other has. As we marry Christ we are co-heirs immediately with Him. As we relate to each other, the Spirit of God will put some of us together so that inheritances will be combined. Paul shared in Timothy's inheritance in Christ, and Timothy shared in Paul's. We effectively combine our pieces of pie, but there is no sorrow or harm accompanying it.

Wherever and whenever any leader tries to move a landmark in the kingdom of God, I am convinced that a curse will surely come. God promises it! It can be repented of, but the ripples of mistrust and hurt go out and can not be easily stopped, if at all. We must be terribly careful in these matters of authority, for all authority belongs to Him. Ambition is at the root of all such attempts. Satan removed a landmark in the garden. Christ had to die on the cross to restore it. Wrong ambition is devilish indeed.

CHAPTER

20

THE MYSTERY OF
LAWLESSNESS

"For the mystery of lawlessness is already at work" (II Thess. 2:7)

The Bible reveals that the entire world is steeped in the mystery of lawlessness. That is because the whole world lies in the power of wickedness (I John 5:19). Unfortunately, the church is not exempt from the influence of wickedness. There is more lawlessness in the world today because there are more people than ever before. Lawlessness is in the heart of man. One expression of lawlessness, anarchy, is very much alive today in the Body of Christ. Since the emergence of the people of God on the earth the mystery of lawlessness has manifested in its various forms.

In the book of Joshua we see this mystery of lawlessness at work in the hearts of men in the days following the death of Joshua. The writer sums up that period by stating that "every man did what was right in his own eyes" (Judges 17:6). This was certainly a wrong concept, but it was rooted in that mystery of lawlessness that was at work in the earth.

Manifestations in the Church

There have been many different manifestations of lawlessness in the Church. One form it has taken in recent decades is in so-called "co-equality" or "co-equal eldership". This is a form of local church leadership where there is no acknowledged head but rather a group of "co-equal" elders governing the church. It is interesting to note that after the death of Joshua this is exactly the form of government that led Israel; there was no headship but only elders leading as a group. This was the form of government in place just prior to the total break-down that led to anarchy at the time of the Judges (Joshua 24). This is far better than anarchy, but when attempted often produces agendas, gridlock, and lack of vision. This is certainly a wrong method and is often spawned by a spirit of lawlessness that rebels against the blueprint of proper headship as revealed in the scriptures..

Another expression of lawlessness in the church today is usurpation. Foreseen by the apostle Paul, he warned the church at Ephesus of its danger (Acts 20:29-30). There have always been men seeking to gain entrance into a church or group of churches with a view to taking over leadership or cutting away individuals from ordained authority. It is usually the ambitious who succumb to these men and follow them as mentioned in the last chapter. Ambition calls unto ambition as deep calls unto deep. Perhaps the Lord uses these men to weed out of the church those whose hearts easily go astray. Nevertheless, the resulting trauma caused by these men is painful and often cripples the work of God. The divisions that these men cause can impede for years the faith of those that are weak or who are babes in Christ.

A Story of Usurpation

There was a dear friend of mine in a foreign land. After twenty years the Lord had put together several wonderful churches under his apostolic leadership. The anointing and blessing of the Lord was evident. As is often the case, the evidences of successful ministry began to attract those who wanted to illegally partake of the fruit. Many came in their integrity because they saw the apostolic anointing on the brother. Others came only because they saw ministry opportunities and because of a desire to steal from the tree. Like David in 1 Chr 12:1, my friend welcomed them all . He was a careful but accepting man, willing to let the Holy Spirit do the sorting.

One of the new men that came into the group had a big church and a very charismatic presence. It was clear from the beginning that he came with ideas of leadership that didn't always include the faithful apostolic brother. At about this time a large, aggressive and expanding apostolic network from the United States also moved in, attracted by the plum hanging on the tree and desiring that the faithful apostolic man would join with them along with the several churches that he had pioneered and attracted. It became quickly clear that a pyramidal organization was being built rather than solid relationships. They were acquiring churches. He was being added to the "down line". When he resisted the efforts to make him a part of the large organization, they went elsewhere, but took with them both the charismatic leader with the large church and one other church. Both of these churches were among the wealthiest and most promising in terms of numbers and dollar income.

Upon one of their leaders being confronted by me for going in and tearing up this flock, the answer was given that "they didn't divide the work, it was the 'ambition' of the charismatic leader who followed them that divided the work." Now this was actually a true analysis of what happened. But lawlessness and ambition in the heart of one man will call unto lawlessness and ambition in the heart of another man, just as "deep calls unto deep." The damage was done. Relationships were strained. The work was temporarily weakened. Also it should be noted here that the larger group which enticed the two churches to follow them eventually had their own major problems. Ambition has built in seeds of destruction. Christ will not bless the wrong kind of ambition.

Many pastors will accept disgruntled members from other churches without question within the same town or neighborhood. This is tantamount to encouraging lawlessness. Often it transfers sin and lawlessness from one group or church to another. May the Lord give us faithful people and fellow workers who will not succumb to the spirit of lawlessness.

God's Gift of Leaders

One of the reasons God gives leaders is to safeguard the church from the spirit of lawlessness. That's because true leaders will keep the saints properly directed to the true Shepherd rather than to them selves. This is exactly what the apostle Paul advocated concerning those who would try to usurp authority in the Body of Christ "in order to draw away disciples after them" (Acts 20:27). When ambitious leaders themselves usurp authority and role model lawlessness, there

111

is little hope for much to happen other than pain and division. A true apostle will always resist such men.

Just as the Father gave the Son (John 3:16), the Son in turn gave to the Church certain gifts, the so-called "five-fold ministry" (Ephesians 4:11). Its purpose is to form, equip and guide the church, to serve the church, and to bring its members corporately to maturity so it can fulfill its God-given destiny and purpose. These gifted men are precisely anointed for that purpose and have true authority from heaven. It stands to reason therefore that one of the results of their authority is to cause the hearts of men to be tested as does all authority that comes down from above. For example, true apostolic authority will often bring out rebellion in hearts; not solely for the purpose of exposing it but that in exposing it, it might be put away. When the authority of God is exercised properly by apostles it should have the effect of exposing and destroying all rebellion against the King that exists in the Body of Christ. Ephesians 4 is partly lifted from Ps 68:18 which says that:

> *"Thou hast ascended on high, thou hast led captivity captive, thou hast received gifts for men, yea, for the rebellious also, that the Lord might dwell among them." (KJV)*

The Holy Spirit raises up elders and other ministries in the Church (Acts 20:28), but Christ Himself personally calls apostles (and the other five-fold ministry gifts). Several passages make it clear that the apostle is called directly by Christ (Romans 1:1, I Cor 1:1, II Timothy 1:11). It also seems to indicate that there is a witness among the people (or at least should be) when they are taught to recognize a true apostle.

The Anointing Cannot Be Acquired

According to the apostle Paul, the very foundation of the church is put in place by the apostolic -prophetic team (Eph 2:20; 3:5). With the office comes the anointing to function in that particular sphere which is given by Christ. This anointing cannot be acquired by study or obtaining degrees or even by prayer. It is a sovereign choice and act of God. "He gave some..." It is supernatural, not natural. It may be accompanied with administrative or executive ability, but often is not. Worldly ability has no bearing on it, but may enhance and adorn it if it is present and subservient to it. It comes from Jesus Christ and is part of the overall anointing which flows from Him. The early church was built upon apostolic doctrine and anointing, and New Testament churches must continue to be built on that doctrine and anointing today, for Christ is the same yesterday, today and forever (Hebrews 13:8).

That is not to say that any new apostolic doctrine is being formed today, for it is not. At the close of the book of Revelation the apostle John warns that no one should add or subtract from the words of the book (Rev. 22:18-19). There is no doubt that the Holy Spirit is referring to the Word of God, canonized much later but known to Him even then. What is written in Scripture is all that there is to be written and no apostle was to come along to add or take away anything from the written revelation. We only continue to receive new light and revelation on that Scripture.

Honest Men Continue to Struggle

While honest men have struggled for almost two thousand years over certain interpretations of that Word, it doesn't change the nature of that Word. There is room for honest differences between those of good heart. What we can be assured of is that the Holy Spirit will lead us into all truth before it is all over if we remain honest, teachable, and humble. For those interested in a deeper study of this premise, I highly recommend *Purpose Directed Theology, Getting Our Priorities Right in Evangelical Controversies* by Darrell L. Bock.[1]

God demands that apostles, above all other ministries, exhibit a lack of guile as a necessary ingredient of their ministry. Paul brilliantly outlines our ministry in 2 Cor 4-6. His number one point is integrity in the Word.

"But we have renounced the hidden things of shame, not walking in craftiness nor handling the word of God deceitfully, but by manifestation of the truth commending ourselves to every man's conscience in the sight of God" (2 Cor. 4:2)

1 Intervarsity Press, Downers Grove, IL, 2002.

The Problem of False Apostles

Last but not least of the problems in the modern church associated with lawlessness is that of false apostles. According to the apostle Paul in II Cor. 11:13-15, false apostles are not only deceitful workers, but agents of Satan (even though perhaps unwittingly). These men sought glory, money, and authority for themselves as well as preached false doctrine not in keeping with the sound doctrine upon which the church is built.

It is no wonder then that in commending the church at Ephesus, the risen Christ pointed out that they "cannot bear those who are evil. And you have tested those who say they are apostles and are not, and have found them liars" (Revelation 2:2). This is almost the first thing he says to the first church he talks to among the seven. It has to be foundationally important.

Only true apostles can lay out, plant, and maintain true church foundations. If the foundation is not true the building will be skewed. Legalism instead of true holiness is often caused by a faulty foundation.

I am blessed with two sons who are building contractors. Some years ago, one of them was called by a desperate contractor. He had just fired his framing subcontractor. The building frame was up and the roof was partially on when he discovered that the whole building was badly out of plumb, though the foundation was square. My son was hired to see if he could possibly fix it. It was comical, heroic and sad, all at the same time, to see his men pulling and tugging on the walls of that building. They loosened certain parts of the wall. They had two heavy pick-up trucks chained to sections of the wall pulling to move the walls but not break them. At one point one of the trucks lifted slightly off the ground for a moment. After a full day's work, they had it almost plumb enough to pass inspection and satisfy the contractor. Had the foundation been off, it would have been impossible to correct the problem.

As any contractor will tell you, it is difficult, if not impossible, to correct a building already constructed upon a skewed foundation. But let us not despair! All is not lost. The Holy Spirit is one Contractor that can true up a foundation, even after construction of the building has begun. Yet He uses true apostles and true prophets to do the job.

CHAPTER

21

THE NEED FOR HELP

"Counsel in the heart of man is like deep water, but a man of understanding will draw it out." *(Prov 20:5)*

A story told by an old man years ago down in Eastern North Carolina illustrates the mentality of some brethren. He told of a farmer who lived on an island in the Roanoke River. This old farmer was very proud of his island for it had excellent land for growing crops. He lived there alone with his chickens, cows and dogs on a beautiful little farm.

One day a group from up the river came to see him to warn him of an impending flood. "There have been torrential rains up in the hills and the flood is coming this way. Get off the island while you still can!" The old man refused to budge, saying he would stick it out on his island. He had been there all of his life and had survived floods before. Besides, he knew the Lord wouldn't let him down. The Lord would protect him.

The river rose steadily until the old man had to get on his roof. A neighbor came by in a rowboat and offered to take him off the island, which was by now under water. The old man refused saying, "The Lord will not let me down, He will save me! Praise the Lord."

An hour or so later another neighbor came by in a powerboat with the same scenario. Again the old man insisted the Lord would save him. Finally a National Guard helicopter arrived and offered to swing him from the roof, which was now within an inch or two of being totally submerged. Again the answer was the same, "The Lord will save me."

Several minutes later the old man was swept to his death by drowning. Upon reaching heaven, he reproached the Lord. "I put all my faith in you and you didn't save me" was his embittered accusation. With wonderful patience the Lord looked him right in the eye and said, "I heard you, and I sent three people to save you, but you refused."

We have to want help and be humble enough to foster the relationships that will provide covering and help in the time of need. Fortunately, there are many lone pastors and independent brethren in the Kingdom today who are sincerely looking for fellowship and identity. This is undoubtedly a result of the moving of the Spirit of God. Many have come to understand their vulnerability in standing alone. They know that real effectiveness is the result of being part of a larger group. Thus, the Spirit of God is creating a great yearning for unity and this is certainly a good thing.

Scripture gives many examples of the importance of working with others as well as the dangers inherent in remaining alone. Perhaps the most poignant example is found in the book of Judges and the story of the people of Laish:

> "So they...went to Laish, to a people quiet and secure; and they struck them with the edge of the sword and burned the city with fire. There was no deliverer, because it was far from Sidon, and they had no ties with anyone"
> *(Judges 18:27-28 Emphasis mine)*

The people of Laish were peaceful, minding their own business and by all accounts were independent and happy. Undoubtedly, they never considered that a day would come when they would need help from outside. Yet that day did come and there was no deliverance, because they were far from help (Sidon) and they had no ties with anyone.

Scripture is clear that the more dedicated a man or woman is and the more aligned with God's purposes, the more the enemy will target him or her. This is especially true for leaders and their churches. He will attack wherever he finds a weak point, unhealed wound or unconfessed sin. Satan and his demonic forces hate the Church and every believer in it. He especially hates shepherds, for he would like to scatter the flock.

One of the ways God has ordered for our protection from the enemy is to receive help from the brethren. The Body of Christ is made up of many parts, gifts, and levels of understanding. The members of the Body need each other (see I Corinthians 12:14-26 and Ephesians 4:7-16). These Scriptures are to be fulfilled in each local church as its members function together and through five-fold ministry relationships.

Yet even though we are technically members of the Body, we can be alone in the battle. When David sought Uriah's death he devised a plan whereby he would die in battle by the hand of the enemy (II Samuel 11:14-15). David knew he could achieve Uriah's death by ordering him into the gate where the battle was fiercest and simultaneously ordering Joab to withdraw support from around him. Uriah's fate was sealed. Chances for our survival are slim if we are alone in the midst of the battle. Yet that is exactly the situation that many leaders find them-selves in today—alone in the midst of the battle. This does not mean they have no acquaintances. It means they have not developed relationships of depth,trust and unity sufficient to achieve a true covering.

To look a positive example, Saul's first act as king of Israel was to rally all Israel to save the men of Jabesh-Gilead (I Samuel 11). Surrounded by the enemy, these men in desperation sent messages to their brethren to come and help them. Saul came and brought Israel with him. What an example of the Body of Christ in action! A great deliverance was wrought as the men of Jabesh-Gilead recognized their limitation and called upon their brethren to help.

Another good example can be seen in the life of David. During his lifetime, David faced many power struggles as well as betrayal by those closest to him. His son Absalom, his son Adonijah, and his nephew, Joab. Yet because he had established a strong relationship with his mighty men they faithfully served him in his time of need. At one point they even rescued him from several giants who would certainly have killed him (II Sam. 15:21). David's relationships with his mighty men are not only a key lesson on the value of being a good leader, but of the need to be rightly related to others in order to take and maintain a kingdom.

Perhaps the writer of Ecclesiastes summed it up best:

> *"Two are better than one, because they have a good reward for their labor. For if they fall, one will lift up his companion. But woe to him who is alone when he falls, for he has no one to help him up. Again, if two lie down together, they will keep warm; but how can one be warm alone? Though one may be overpowered by another, two can withstand him. And a three-fold cord is not quickly broken" (Ecc. 4:9-12)*

In recent years, we have all bemoaned the sad witness of the nationally known ministers who have become public spectacles. As this was happening many pastors have said, "If only he had had a relationship with someone who could speak into his life." Yet very often the fallen brother was proud, independent or cynical and even in crisis could not see the value of counsel and real cover. If he had, he might have avoided falling so hard. Apostolic fathers ought to cultivate such trust and relationships above all.

The Danger of Independence

There are many leaders today who, while recognizing their need for fellowship, don't really want any close relationships that might involve commitment on any level. Some of them have had horrific experiences in the past relating to legal or ambitious men who used them or their churches for their own self-aggrandizement. Many just don't see any need for help or are too proud to admit they don't know everything

But, let us return to Laish. When those who came to Laish to conquer it arrived, this is how they saw the inhabitants of the district:

> *"So the five men departed and went to Laish. They saw the people who were there, how they dwelt safely, in the manner of the Sidonians, quiet and secure. There were no rulers in the land who might put them to shame for anything. They were far from the Sidonians, and they had no ties with anyone" (Judg. 18:7)*

What a picture of a confident people feeling safe and secure with no need for anyone else. There were no rulers (magistrates) in the land to which they were accountable. They had no outside relationships. They lived "like" the Sidonians, but they were far away and had no relationship or accountability to them or anyone. And the truth is, no one else had a relationship or was accountable to them either! No wonder they were such an easy prey.

The fact that the people of Laish dwelt alone and therefore perished is not meant to suggest that outside help will always save the day. Yet it is God's best that we receive help from one another since none of us have all the insights and gifts necessary to solve every problem. Nor do we have ability to perform every task. Solomon perhaps said it best; "Where no counsel is, the people fall; but in the multitude of counselors there is safety" (Proverbs 11:4).

There are special people that God puts into our lives to help us develop in the natural; parents, teachers, coaches, Marine Corp drill instructors, mentors in business and the like. Our progress nearly always depends on our ability to receive, assimilate and put into practice what they can teach us. In the same way, God gives us others to help us in the development of our lives spiritually as well. Just as natural development depends on the assistance of others, so life in God requires those special relationships to guide us in the way. Why would God want us to be independent in our spiritual development? We need to earnestly look therefore and be open to those special relationships that God provides so that we can receive the maximum benefit in our spiritual journey.

Thwarting What God is Doing

One of God's provisions today for churches so that we might avoid being like the men of Laish is the emergence of apostolic networks; groupings of churches working together under apostolic leadership and covering. All across the earth these networks have sprung up promising to provide local churches with spiritual covering and protection. Twice I received invitations from networks to join and become part of them. Usually, the invitation will come from the key man around which this particular group is forming. While many of these networks are legitimate, often they are raw attempts to take advantage of the vulnerability of lonely men and gain their money and use their contacts and other gifts.

So often, men will thwart what God is attempting to do by taking God's idea and running with it in the flesh. In my own day there have been several legitimate moves of the Holy Spirit which have been marred by overly zealous and ambitious men.

God is For Prosperity, Discipleship and Faith

For instance, God really wants discipleship and genuine authority established among his people today. Yet many are wary of pastoral and apostolic oversight because of excesses they experienced in previous movements in earlier decades. The same is true of prosperity and faith. There is no doubt that God intends to bless His people. Yet because of the excesses of a few men and women who lacked understanding and proper balance in the Word of God, much of the Church is leery of the prosperity and word-faith movements and will not even examine the merit in what these brethren offer. This is unfortunate since many of the brethren from those camps know how to access the Spirit of God by faith better than some that have resisted their teachings.

God is For Prophets

The same is true of prophets. God certainly wants to restore real prophets in the church today. They are vital to the church's destiny. They are vital in giving understanding of the times. Yet so much presumption and weirdness has attended the restoration of the prophetic that many reject it. Some, I am afraid, fear it. Many prophets seem to be unaccountable to anyone on earth or in heaven for their excesses.

God desires balance. Whenever one aspect of God's ministry gifts is exalted inordinately there will be trouble. God wants a team, not super prophets and super apostles. Whenever one aspect of God's message to men is presented consistently out of proportion with the rest of the full gospel there will be trouble. Paul said he preached the "full gospel" not just a part of it.

In our day, God desires to restore true apostolic ministry and relationship to churches. Yet once again, some men are taking the ball and running with it in a carnal way. Suffice it to say for now that it is extremely urgent that we who are in leadership do not let this golden opportunity to respond to the Holy Spirit drown in the pools of ambition, opportunism, or greed.

CHAPTER

22

VERTICAL VERSUS HORIZONTAL RELATIONSHIPS

*"Do not forsake your own friend or your father's friend, Nor
go to your brother's house in the day of your calamity; Better
is a neighbor nearby than a brother far away" (Prov 27:10)*

Throughout the world today, there is a great emphasis on unity among pastors and churches in the local setting. This movement is no doubt a work of the Holy Spirit and has produced much fruit in many places. Many local pastors in a great number of cities meet regularly for worship and prayer, and are organizing joint worship, evangelistic and youth ventures. Many are overcoming historical denominational barriers, as well as cultural and racial barriers to present a unified face to the principalities, powers, as well as the unsaved.

These relationships of pastor to pastor and church to church in cities and localities may be best described as horizontal relationships. They are occurring despite differences of background, origin, vision and doctrine. They are beneficial in many ways, but especially in the fact that they tend to pool the strengths and gifts resident in the local churches. The result is that much more is accomplished in the Kingdom of God locally.

Regional groupings of churches can develop young leaders and launch them into national and international ministries through their various vertical connections (which we will discuss in a moment). When trouble occurs, these churches are in a better position to help each other quickly. They are able to strengthen new church plants together. A lot of good work in and for the Kingdom of God is accomplished through these horizontal relationships.

Vertical Relationships

On the other hand, the New Testament reveals that there are also vertical relationships as well as horizontal. These vertical relationships involve authority, oversight, protection, identity and those distinctions that make us different from each other. They include sameness of vision, cultural backgrounds, denominational origins, and the like. They include father-son relationships. In modern lingo, it can be said that they have the same DNA. Perhaps one simple way of viewing this is that horizontal relationships are regional, neighbor-to-neighbor relationships while vertical are essentially "family." Churches and leaders have had a tendency to organize vertically because of background, history, doctrine, relationships and vision..

"Plastic" Vertical Relationships Make Horizontal Relationships Seem More Meaningful

Because of lack of true fathering apostles, "plastic", hierarchical vertical relationships have resulted. There are many situations that the ministry and quasi-covering that takes place in the horizontal relationships seem far more meaningful to some struggling young leaders than those encountered in the vertical.

It is quite obvious that both types of relationships are good and are in the plan of God. Paul's ministerial relationships to Timothy, Titus and to Aquilla and Priscilla as well as to the churches he planted and nurtured were essentially vertical in nature. The trip to Jerusalem in Acts 15 to settle the legalism question worked through vertical relationships. Paul's and Barnabas' relationship to the church at Antioch was vertical. The relationship of the men of Jabesh-Gilead to Saul was vertical (I Samuel 11:1-11), and this is indeed what saved them from their enemies when the crisis came.

Holding Both in Balance

The will of God is that we hold both types of relationships in balance. We must receive what is passed down through the apostolic fathers and their teams through vertical relationships;

> *"And the things that you have heard from me among many witnesses, commit these to faithful men who will be able to teach others also" (II Timothy 2:2).*

In this passage Timothy was to take what he received from the apostle Paul and pass it on to others. This is clearly a vertical relationship. Paul also told Timothy to "stir up the gift of God which is in you through the laying on of my hands", another clear reference to the vertical kind of relationship. It is clear that vertical relationships were vital in the ministry of the apostle Paul and his disciples.

Don't Sacrifice One for the Other

The danger always lies in sacrificing one set of relationships for the other. To exalt or over emphasize any of God's truths, ministry, callings or gifts over the others is to be out of balance. In the father-son or vertical relationship there is a blessing that involves strengthening, covering, identity, and protection that cannot be substituted for in horizontal relationships. *It is a spiritual matter, not an intellectual one. It is a question of what God will do through the relationship, not what man will do.*

Do you see why it is so important that there be real fathering apostles in the Body of Christ? If there are not, then a unique and certain channel of blessing, unity and strength is missing. A true apostle will encourage his sons to form greater and greater horizontal relationships while doing everything possible to strengthen vertical relationships at the same time.

It is time to draw the horizontal circle bigger, not smaller. I have never forgotten a poem my wife introduced to me more than fifty years ago that neatly expresses what our attitude should be:

"He drew a circle that shut me out...
Heretic, rebel, a thing to flout...
But love and I had the wit to win...
We drew a circle that took him in!"
                                        Anonymous

CHAPTER 22

CHAPTER

23

THE ELIJAH TO JEHU ANOINTING

"the Lord is a Man of War" (Exod 15:3)

"Thus Jehu destroyed Baal from Israel"
(2Ki 10:28)

"The Lord shall go forth like a mighty man; He
shalL stir up His zeal like a man of war. He shall
cry out, yes, shout aloud; He shall prevail against
His enemies"
(Isa 42:13)

In the introduction to this book I briefly mentioned the importance of the concluding prophecy of the Old Testament contained in the book of Malachi (4:5-6). This very important prophecy sets the stage for the Second Coming of the Lord. It speaks of the sending of Elijah before the great and terrible day. Besides the specific promise of the return in glory of our Lord Himself, there is no more exciting prophecy in the entire Word of God.

The importance of this prophecy cannot be overestimated since it contains what might be properly called the "last words" of the Old Testament. If a man's last words are important how much more the last words of God at the end of an age? A person will usually say something relatively important when speaking his final words to those he loves. In the same sense, these final words of the Old Testament include some of God's most important thoughts.

The heart of this prophecy is the promise of God to send "Elijah the prophet before the coming of the great and dreadful day of the Lord" who would "turn the hearts of the fathers to the children, and the hearts of the children to their fathers." In Luke's Gospel we are clearly told how these words were fulfilled in the appearance of John the Baptist whose coming was in the "spirit and power of Elijah (Luke 1:17). Even so, the prophecy still has important implications for the time before the Second Appearing of Jesus Christ, the restoration of father-son relationships in the church today and what I shall call the "Elijah to Jehu anointing", There are resultant implications for spiritual warfare today.

My aim in this final chapter is to underscore an important principle central to the restoration of apostles; *the need for spiritual fathers to understand God's plan and to have the ability to pass on that vision and have it enacted by their sons and grandsons.* That is to say, while God raises up fathering apostles who in turn are given great vision for the Church, they must not think that they themselves are to do it all. God's plan is that they would properly prepare the next generation so that when they are taken off the scene what they saw and lived for is being lived out in their spiritual sons. To apply this principle we shall look briefly at the history of the prophet Elijah and the relationship he had with his spiritual son Elisha and spiritual grandson Jehu who carried on his ministry after he was gone.

Elijah Anoints Elisha

In the book of First Kings, Elijah appeared at a time of great spiritual danger. The worship of Baal was rampant. Jezebel reigned with her husband Ahab. God was to use Elijah to bring Israel back to the Lord. Yet many of the things he was told to do and longed to see in his lifetime did not occur. Rather, God reserved them for his spiritual son Elisha and others to accomplish.

After Elijah defeated the prophets of Baal at Carmel he fled from Jezebel who threatened his life. Passing through the wilderness, he came to Horeb, the mountain of God. There, God met Elijah and commissioned him to perform three tasks:

> *"Then the Lord said to him: "Go return on your way to the Wilderness of Damascus; and when you arrive, (1) anoint Hazael as king over Syria. Also you shall (2) anoint Jehu the son of Nimshi as king over Israel. And (3) Elisha the son of Shaphat of Abel Meholah you shall anoint as prophet in your place." (1 Kings 19:15-16)*

Looking at Elijah's history we find that he only performed one of these tasks during his lifetime—anointing Elisha to be his replacement. This is quite amazing. At a time in his life when he felt like running from his duties, apparently losing his confidence in God and himself, he was met by the Almighty, given the key to destroying the very enemy from whom he was running, and he failed to carry it out. We would probably call him a failure today. We might say he lacked faith.

We know that God didn't look at it this way. Elijah later appeared on the Mount of Transfiguration with Jesus, which can hardly be construed as a reward for failure. James tells us that Elijah was a man with the same human frailty that we all have. It wasn't that Elijah had failed at all; God had simply desired that his vision, mission and 'spirit' be passed on to a son who would in turn, communicate that same spirit to other sons. They would complete the task. If Elijah equipped his sons and they performed, he would be successful.

The Bible narrative is clear that Elisha actually received the mantle of Elijah as he saw him ascend to heaven in a whirlwind (2 Kings 2:11-12). As Elisha cried, "My father, my father, the chariot of Israel and the horsemen thereof", he took the mantle of Elijah and began to carry out his vision.

An Encouraging Prophecy

Many years ago I received a prophetic utterance from a man whom I respect very much. It stated that although I would produce a small amount of fruit in my lifetime, my sons and grandsons would produce a far greater amount of fruit

than I. This prophecy did little for my sense of self importance at the time, but I have come to cherish it.

One of my spiritual sons has developed as an true apostle in a foreign country. Several years ago I had the reward and privilege of visiting him on the field. As I watched him teaching the young students from remote mountain tribes in their native tongue, God spoke to me. Although I knew none of them personally, God witnessed to me in that moment that they were my grand sons. They were imbibing some of the 'spirit' and vision that I had imparted to my spiritual son. Who knows how far they will go and what they will do for the Lord in their life times? I had a vision for this particular country, but I understood that I would never personally carry it out. *We don't have to perform everything the Lord has let us envision!* We can inspire and equip those who can! Our sons and grandsons can!

Of the Increase of His Government, There Shall Be No End

That Elisha received Elijah's mantle is amply proved. There were two other tasks that God commanded Elijah to do. Elisha later carried these out. Elisha anointed Hazael as king of Syria (2 Kings 8:7-13) Through his servant, a young prophet, he anointed Jehu as king over Israel (2 Kings 11:1-10). Thus, even though Elijah himself did not directly perform these acts, through his son and grandsons he fulfilled all that the Lord had commanded him.

Reading the entire story of Elisha in the book of Second Kings we discover that the anointing on Elisha far exceeded that of his predecessor. Having received a 'double portion' of Elijah's spirit, Elisha performed far more miracles than Elijah. And in a sense, the young, unnamed son of a prophet who anointed Jehu was a spiritual grandson of Elijah. Thus, it is accurate to say that the Word of God traces at least two generations of spiritual sons' of Elijah who filled with his spirit, anointing and vision, fulfilled the original vision that God had given to their spiritual father.

What if Elijah had failed to anoint Elisha to succeed him? I think it is clear that without Elisha being designated as Elijah's successor, one of the most important spiritual victories in Israel would not have occurred. For it was in fact Jehu , in a sense another grandson, whom Elisha anointed who finally defeated Jezebel and thus fulfilled the calling of Elijah to rid Israel of Jezebel's whoredoms and her controlling spirit (2 Kings 9:30-36).

Much has been written and preached of late concerning the spirit of Jezebel. This spirit manifests itself in many churches today as a spirit of rebellion and control whose aim is to emasculate all true authority in God's house. Elijah may have felt like he failed in his own day but God had a plan to use one of his own spiritual sons to carry out His purpose to rid the land of Jezebel.

Thus, the anointing upon Elijah was transferred to his son, Elisha and then to his grandson, the young prophet who in turn anointed Jehu. It was this Jehu who destroyed the enemies of God and thus fulfilled the initial vision of Elijah.

The Warrior Anointing, A Need for Today

Jehu had a warrior's anointing to hate evil and stand up for good. How desperately needed this is today in the body of Christ. Not that we want to mirror Jehu completely, for this man produced much mayhem and carnage. Yet the attitude of heart and spirit in Jehu is desperately needed today in the church. It is an anointing for warfare to war against the enemies of God and defeat them. It is Christ-like, in that "the Lord is a man of war".

Jehu also had another anointing which we need in the church today. He was indeed a warrior and a zealot. But he had something else. As he rode into town that day to carry out his call, Jezebel came out on a high balcony to meet him. She was seductively attired and had a certain worldly aura. She must have been very seductive indeed. She was surrounded by several of her eunuchs (2 Kings 9:32). These eunuchs were by definition emasculated men. They could not produce fruit. It was not possible for them to be fathers. Emasculated men usually gravitate to the spirit of Jezebel. They were her servants. They were under her influence and control. She was a wicked queen. Do not forget that she had arranged the death of a man just to acquire a piece of land for her husband. She had inspired fear in the prophet Elijah. These eunuchs were hers to command.

But Jehu looked up and asked, "Who is on my side? Who?" The Holy Spirit then reveals to us that two or three of these eunuchs looked out on Jehu. Then Jehu commanded, "Throw her down! They threw her down! Imagine that! Something powerful happened to these men. They were no longer under her control. They became men again. As they gazed at Jehu, a powerful transforming anointing overcame them and changed them from eunuchs into activated servants of God. I call this "The Jehu anointing." This anointing has to do with true influence that is the key to leadership. However you care to analyze it, we need it.

I believe that as the spirit of Elijah raises up and enables apostles to be real spiritual fathers in these days, and as they impart to their sons and grand sons the vision of the Coming King and His Kingdom, marvelous things will begin to happen. Not only will there be great warriors, but there will be those who will have the anointing to wake up the eunuchs in the church. Many men are asleep, emasculated if you will. When this anointing is manifested, men will begin to take their rightful places in families and churches. Their level of commitment to God, church, wives and children will jump.

The Spirit of Elijah Today

The story of Elijah and the continuation of his ministry through his son Elisha has much instruction for us today. When most people talk about the spirit of Elijah they are referring to the miracles of this man of God and the many exploits which he did. And we certainly should for this mighty man did many notable exploits.

Yet when Malachi refers to the appearing of Elijah before the Lord returns he does not refer to his miracles or mighty power but to his fathering ministry. It is that aspect of this man's ministry that chiefly will characterize the days before the return of the Lord. We should expect that right up until the Lord's coming there will be a manifestation of Elijah's spirit "turning the hearts of the fathers to the children and the children to the fathers."

When apostles in our day begin to move in the spirit of Elijah, the results will be the raising up of powerful sons in their stead. *The blessing of life mentioned earlier in this book will then flow from the fathers to these sons and daughters and hence into the church.*

The anointing for warfare, the "Jehu anointing," will also settle on some sons and daughters as well. What is God's purpose in this? One of things He intends to do is to use Elijah once again to destroy Jezebel in His house. We are obviously not talking about literal Jezebel since she has been dead and gone for centuries. The dogs ate her! Yet according to Scripture the spirit of Jezebel lives on in many churches and must be dealt with (Rev. 2:20).

CONCLUSION

This completes our exploration into the subject of the heart of the Apostle. We have seen that the heart of an apostle should be a father's heart first of all. I have shown the importance and relevance of fathers and sons coming into divine alignment as the age closes. We have seen how true prosperity, blessing and life itself flows out of the correct and godly application of fatherhood to the church.

We explored some of the reasons apostles have made it so difficult for sons to properly relate to them and have shown what God would like to see as the heart of a true apostle. I have equated all of this to the emerging role of the apostolic ministry, which the Holy Spirit is releasing upon the earth today. We wish to see the church prosperous and blessed.

I have urged sons and daughters for their own sakes to relate properly to fathers even though those fathers may fall short. We touched on the benefits that occur as a result of so honoring the principle of fatherhood.

While trying to give a benchmark for young churches and leaders to measure against when sizing up men who call themselves apostles, at the same time it was the aim of this book to suggest that apostles ought to use the same benchmark to size themselves up. We should measure ourselves against the desires and guidelines of the Lord. Christianity is primarily a "heart" religion. What is in the heart is paramount to Christ. This is what He looks at when ultimately qualifying anyone for leadership. This should be our holy attitude for the sake of the Lord and His children. Everything is at stake! After all, didn't Malachi say, " and he (the spirit of Elijah) will turn the hearts of the fathers to the children, and the hearts of the children to their fathers, lest I come and strike the earth with a curse?" The hearts are to be turned, not the functions or the positions. This book has majored on the aspects of the heart for that reason. For if the heart is right before God and man, everything else will happen as it should.

May the Lord turn all of our hearts more and more toward each other and toward His great purposes as we see the day approaching. Lord Jesus, may you raise up many real apostles in our day.

Maranatha! (Come Lord Jesus)

Printed in the USA
CPSIA information can be obtained
at www.ICGtesting.com
JSHW082214140824
68134JS00014B/626